MONSTER POETRY

Poems From The Home Counties

Edited by Donna Samworth

First published in Great Britain in 2014 by:
Young Writers
Remus House
Coltsfoot Drive
Peterborough
PE2 9BF
Telephone: 01733 890066
Website: www.youngwriters.co.uk

Book Design by Ashley Janson

ISBN 978-1-78203-833-7
Printed and bound in the UK by BookPrintingUK
Website: www.bookprintinguk.com

Foreword

Young Writers was established in 1991, dedicated to encouraging reading and creative writing by young people. Our nationwide writing initiatives are designed to inspire ideas and the incentive to write, and in turn develop literacy skills and confidence, whilst participating in a fun, imaginative activity. The final reward is the opportunity for the budding young writer to see their work in print.

Our latest competition, *Monster Poetry*, focuses on uncovering the different techniques used in poetry and encouraging pupils to explore new ways to write a poem. Using a mix of imagination, expression and poetic styles, this anthology is an impressive snapshot of the inventive, original and skilful writing of young people today. We hope this collection will delight readers for years to come.

Contents

St Mary Star Of The Sea Roman Catholic Primary School, St Leonards-On-Sea

St Meryl School, Watford

The Poems

In Monster Land

In Monster Land the monsters have different personality,
Monsters roar, monsters write, monsters have agility.
In Monster land the monsters are different shapes and sizes,
Some are big, some are small and some have big incisors.
In Monster Land the monsters are lots of different types,
Some called Lilks, some called Barfs, and some are even named as Snypes
In Monster Land the monsters creep into some bedrooms,
But they don't go into kitchens they're afraid of the big brooms!

India Jarman-Tew (9)

Cookie Friend

Bamboozl comes from planet Cookie,
He flies around space,
One day he flew around and around
And found planet Earth.
He didn't know what it was,
He landed with a crash,
His head spinning round and round,
He feels something under his feet,
It's something green and glossy,
He looks up from the ground,
Bang!
Walks straight into a boy called James.
Takes a look and runs away,
Bamboozl screams with a snap,
And then Offers his hand,
Bamboozl asks:
'Do you have any cookies?'
James says, 'Over at my house,'
The boy takes him to his house,
Brings him to the deep dark room called the kitchen,
There laid a pile of cookies,
Under a beaming light,
Bamboozl scoffs them up!
'Yummy,' says Bamboozl,
James says, 'He's my cookie friend.'
Off Bamboozl goes back to Planet Cookie.

Ilja

Making Monsters

Based On 'Making Monsters' By Gavin Stewart

Vampular the monster
I made up last week
A monster so scary
I'm now losing sleep.

My monster has
A body like a human
Eyes as sharp as lions teeth
He has skin as black as a bat
Feet like claws.

My monster is
As scary as a vampire
As loud as a lion's roar
As clever as a teacher
As smelly as a stinky ditch.

Vampular the monster
I made up last week
A monster so scary
I'm now losing sleep.

Emily (7)

Google Goes To The North Pole

One day I was playing in the snow,
Until I heard a creature 'Ho!'
I looked round my shoulder,
Then next to a big boulder
There was a tiny funny monster.
His fur as blue as the sky,
His spots as purple as pie.
His horns as green as a Christmas tree,
And his stripes as orange as tea.
The sign next to him said North Pole,
So I followed him into the cold.
There was a cottage with Santa,
Sat on a chair drinking Fanta!
It's quite strange may I say,
But it's lucky not to pay!
When we went into the house,
We saw a small elf,
On a high shelf!
Santa handed me a new phone,
And said welcome to your new home.

Emilie Prout

The Monster Gang!

There are three monsters I want you to meet,
Which eat anything including your feet!

Squishy is one,
Which squeezing him is a lot of fun,
He is green with two big feet,
And his diet is meat, meat and meat!

Larry is two,
He's covered in goo!
He loves his toys,
And doesn't play with any of the boys!
16 feet high 2 centimetres wide,
And his diet is potatoes, beef, with coleslaw on the side!

The last one is Ben,
Who lives in a rabbit den!
He plays with a Jack in the box,
And his hobby is trying to hit humans with rocks!
He is always hungry and very fat!
And his favourite food is a big fat juicy cat!

So you met the crew,
And I hope I gave you a little clue,
But they are not the most innocent of all . . .
Because they drive me up the wall.

Keziah Williams (10)

The Tlend

Based On 'Making Monsters' By Gavin Stewart

The Tlend was born in the mountains
It has blue and red skin and a purple mouth.
Brown and green eyes, a orange tail and a purple and green arms
The Tlend climbed over the bushes
Its big black foot banged down on the playground.
The trees leant back with fright.
It was walking across the playground to the school.
It's trying to ruin the school.
Children were running everywhere trying to get to the hall
The children ran out and threw water over the Tlend.
It didn't work, they got more water.
They threw it and the Tlend was shrivelling away.
'I'll get you,' said the Tlend
'Hooray, we saved the day!'

Sadie Connolly

My Monster Poem

In a crystal cave far away lay
A monster called Flake. I found her and took her to see the world.

We went to a carnival but
Didn't want to almost die on the roller coasters.

We decided that the carnival
Was not much fun, so we ate a big bun.

We went to a swimming pool.
It was like a shark tank, we jumped in
But poor Flake had sunk.

Flake had a good day, and said she would see me another day.

Anna Gilbert (10)
Auriol Junior School, Epsom

Stitch

Stitch is very hairy and his favourite food is milk dairy
And he is pink and furry
And he likes the smell of dairy.

One cold winter's day he popped out to say
'It's my time to play on this cold winter's day.'

He sometimes pops out from time to time
To say hello and wave goodbye.

Lucy (10)
Auriol Junior School, Epsom

The Unbelievably Dumb Monster Splatty

He said he was from Planet Stupidor.
I believed him straightaway.
He grew two brains when his planet exploded,
But somehow he's even dumber.
He walked around the USA where everyone understood him,
He had a great friend in the President of the USA.

The day he came to England, everything went wrong,
He got run over twenty times and said 1+1 was 8004.
He said he wanted to fly back to America
But when he tried he drove my car into the Atlantic.

He's now recovering . . . in the morgue
His name was Splatty.

Sam Featherstone (10)
Auriol Junior School, Epsom

Candy Floss

Hi to you all
Candy Floss is my name
I'm bright pink on the outside
And lips red as a flame.

I have purple spots
My eyes are green
And it has been said
I look supreme.

I am always fun
And never sad
When I am around
People are always glad.

I love having sleepovers
Because I have lots of friends
We give each other makeovers
And look at the latest trends.

I live on a planet
Not far away
It's covered in sweets
That I snack on all day.

It was lovely to meet you
But now I must fly
My spaceship is ready
So for now goodbye.

Holly Fisher (10)
Auriol Junior School, Epsom

Spongebob Fluffy Pants Meets The Queen

Spongebob Fluffy Pants lives in the air
In a cardboard box,
Putting on his fluffy pants
And his odd woolly socks.

Spongebob Fluffy Pants went for a walk
Fell off his cloud and he fell right down,
Unlucky for him the horse riding was on
He landed in Epsom Downs.

He decided to get on a bus
To London city,
He got pushed off the back
Oh what a pity!

After a couple of days and B&B's
He ended up in Westminster
He went inside Parliament,
And met the Prime Minister.

The Prime Minister gave him a lift
To show the Queen,
The fluffy pants monster
That he had just seen.

When he arrived with the Queen
Mr Fluffy Pants said,
'You're old and bold
And have a very wrinkly head.'

The Queen got mega angry
And called for the royal navy,
As soon as they arrived
He splatted them with the cook's finest gravy.

She ordered them to drown him
But it never seemed to work,
He pulled himself to the bank
And stole a big white Merc.

He found a time machine
And went back to the morning,
To the time he was still sleeping
And he woke up still snoring.

Spongebob Fluffy Pants lives in the air
In a cardboard box,
Putting on his fluffy pants
And his old woolly socks.

Jack Howes (10)
Auriol Junior School, Epsom

Sweetie Queen

Sweetie Queen's friend was not very well
She decided to visit her to make her better.

She wrote it in a letter
'Yes! Of course!' her friend replied
'Come and see me tomorrow!'

Sweetie Queen was so excited
She ordered her best dress to be cleaned
It was stunning
It had gold sparkles which shone brightly in the sun.

She went to sleep dreaming about her friend
When she woke up she had a bubble bath
And put on her stunning dress.

She rushed her breakfast and had to do her hair all over again.
She screeched to a stop
And she flopped onto the hard, cold pavement.

Ouch! she cried and she held her head
As blood dripped on her dress
Now she's in hospital next to her friend.

Rebecca Dakin (10)
Auriol Junior School, Epsom

Romantic Ralph

Hello, my name's Ralph,
I live down South
I'm fuzzy and cool,
I've got one eye,
That's all.
My mum says I'm funny
And my dad says I look like a bunny
One day I went out,
Just walking about
When I saw this hot fuzz
It gave me a buzz!
I bounced up to this girl
She said her name was Pearl.
She looked just like me
Yet she had such long eyelashes,
I'm surprised she could see
She liked my fuzzy style
I said 'Wanna hang 'round mine for a while?'
She said 'OK, where is it, which way?'
I led her back to mine
We got there in no time
We walked up to my front door
I kicked away an apple core
Pearl said 'This is one disgusting place'
That was the last time I saw her pretty face.

Neve Homes (10) & Rosie Bayton (11)
Auriol Junior School, Epsom

There's A Monster Under My Bed

There's a monster under my bed,
he wishes he was dead.
So one day I showed him the world around him
and that's when life changed for me, Jim.

His dark black eyes sparkled in the sun,
as his razor sharp teeth dug into a bun
I felt through his fur as furry as a rug.
Sometimes I think he eats bugs.

I took him to the coconut mall,
we dressed him like he was going to a ball.
We both got a hot dog
but he dropped his in a bog

We went to a cinema
and he nicknamed me Jimina
We watched Monsters Inc.
I hardly ever saw him blink.

We went to a theme park,
he was as stiff as a piece of bark.
We went on lots of rides,
then went to the zoo with a tour guide

We went to the seaside,
he felt sick after going on all those rides.
He enjoyed making a monster castle out of sand,
then we went over to the bandstand and listened to our favourite band

After that long day,
we got in the car and I fell asleep on the way.
I cuddled into his soft fur
and I think I heard him purr.

Natasha Roche (10)
Auricl Junior School, Epsom

My Monsters Day Out

Hi my name is Keith Wisouski
I'm going to the UK, just Mike and me,
We're going to go visit
The famous 'Thorpe Park'.
We're going to be flying
In the pitch-black dark.
We have now landed at Heathrow Airport Terminal 5,
To be quite honest I'm glad we arrived!
We're in our taxi on the way to our destination
We thought this is fun, let's plan our next vacation.
I'm getting hyped up 'cause we're nearly here,
I can't wait to get riding roller coasters
I can't wait to get there and arrive with a cheer!
OK we're here now first ride will be the Swarm,
But we can't go on there because we're too small!
The next ride we will go on will be Stealth
By the end of that ride we had no health.
After riding nearly all the rides,
We took a taxi to our hotel
That only took one stride.
Finally we got to our hotel room
And flopped down on the bed
Apparently it's a place where you rest your head?
Later on I'll face time,
My family back in Australia
Just after I eat my tortilla!

Ruby Bowers (11)
Auriol Junior School, Epsom

Little Monsters

Stupid Stephanie and Dumb Darren,
Their skin was very dry and barren.
Both the freaks came round for tea,
Sadly, it was not to be.
They romped and stomped upon the chairs,
None of them had any cares.
They jumped and ran across the table
And ate as much as they were able.
The monsters rampaged through the night,
Giving all the neighbours a fright.
Stephanie kicked him in the face,
Darren, however, had more grace.
He patted her and then stepped back,
But Stephanie caught him in a sack!
She tied it up with stamps and string
And gave the neighbours' door a ring.
They opened it, then they said,
'Isn't it time to go to bed?'
So Stupid Stephanie walked back home,
Her voice a tired and weary tone.
She turned around, then there stood,
Dumb Darren, clutching some wood.
He bonked her right on the head,
Then the little monster said,
'Now I really think it is, definitely time for bed!'

Karis Baker (10)
Auriol Junior School, Epsom

Me And Polly's Monster Poem

My name is Perry, I have a pet shop.
One of my horses says 'Neigh' as he eats too much hay.

Let me tell you more about me,
My best friend, he is called Lee.
I'm pink and look like an ice rink.
My feet are square like a bear.
My ears are hearts and pointy like darts.

Me and Lee went to the park, we saw Mark,
It was getting really dark, so we have a sleepover with Mark.

In the morning, we were all yawning
And it was pouring with rain
And Mark had a pain,
Well that's all about me.
See ya!

Sophie Foreman & Polly Middleton (11)
Auriol Junior School, Epsom

A Monster's Day

Let me tell you my monsters' names
My monsters' names are Blaze and Flame.
Suddenly they came across a bog,
Then Blaze bonked Flame with a log.
Then they realised they missed lunch
So they went home to get some brunch,
They like eating cake and cheese,
Give them some or they will eat me.
Then they went to the monster shop
They bought some sweets and fizzy pop.
After they went home to play,
They have had such a busy day.

Abby Verdie (10)
Auriol Junior School, Epsom

Blurrea's Bubbling Day

He was born in the London dungeon
He vanishes into air
No one knows what he does there
Cos he always leaves his pear.

He smells of Lynx Temptation
He's a great sensation
He gets wet with condensation.

He likes Alton Towers
Where he has a lot of powers
He zooms through the line
It takes no time
He goes on the Smiler
With a nail filer.

He leaves for his own city
Oh what a pity
He had a great day
It was in May.

Callum Hilton (10)
Auriol Junior School, Epsom

The Monster That Lived In My Loo

He is revolting, inhumane and sickening
To the monster that lives in my loo
He is also two foot two.
He pops out some time for food and a glass of wine
He goes for a stroll from time to time.
On one cold winter's day he popped out to play with,
A young monster called Slink, but she was very pink.
They went to a ball in an amazing hall.
The hall sparkled as the stars twinkled at night.
They danced and danced till it was over,
Together they walked while eating some pork.
He went back to his loo
That is the monster that lived in my loo.

Oliver Finnegan (10)
Auriol Junior School, Epsom

Monsters Can't Dance

Jim was a furry monster
Whose tail was rather slim
But knees were awfully bandy
And legs were rather thin

He was very good at scaring
And breaking off trees
But when he tried to dance around
He buckled at his knees

Now every year in Monster Ville
They hold the monster dance
Where every single monster
Turns up to skip and prance

And this year when the day arrived
Poor Jim felt so sad,
Because when it came to dancing
He was really very bad

The Wellos started waltzing
The Robots rock 'n' rolled
The Aliens danced a tango
Which was elegant and bold

The Cheackers all did a cha-cha
With a very Latin feel,
And eight booboos then teamed up
For a splendid Scottish reel

Jim swallowed bravely
As he walked towards the floor
But the aliens saw him coming
And they soon began to roar

'Hey look at clumsy Jim'
The monsters all laughed,
'You can't dance, you silly fool
Oh Jim, don't be daft!'

Jim simply froze up,
He was rooted to the spot
'They're right,' he thought, 'I'm useless
Oh I feel like such a clot.'

So he crept off the dance floor
And he started walking home,
He'd never felt so sad before
So sad and so alone

Then he found a clearing
And he looked up at the sky,
'The moon can be so beautiful,'
He whispered with a sigh

'Excuse me!' coughed a bird
Who'd seen Jim earlier on,
'But sometimes when you're different
You just need a different song.'

He threw his arms out sideways
And swung them everywhere,
Then he did a backwards somersault
And leapt up in the air.

How is it you can dance like that?
Please Jim tell us how
But Jim simply smiled
And ended at a bow.

Rana Ralton (10)
Auriol Junior School, Epsom

Fearsome Monster

M y monster is as ginormous as a building
O range eyes like brightness and fire of the sun
N ifty tail slithering as a snake on the ground
S pikes as sharp as thorns hanging from a branch
T eeth spiky as talons from a bald eagle
E ating greedily like a male rhinocerous
R oaring as loud as an aeroplane.

Joshua Buxton (11)
Auriol Junior School, Epsom

Spongebob Fluffy Pants Meets The Queen

Spongebob Fluffy Pants lives in the air
In a cardboard box.
Putting on his fluffy pants
And his odd woollen socks.

Spongebob Fluffy Pants went for a walk
And fell off his cloud.
Unlucky for him the horse riding was on
As into Epsom Downs he ploughed.

He decided to get on a bus
To London city.
He got pushed off the back
Oh what a pity!

After a couple of days and B&B's
He ended up in Westminster.
He went into Parliament
And saw the Prime Minister.

The Prime Minister gave him a lift
To show the Queen
The fluffy pants monster
He had just seen.

When he arrived to see the Queen
Mr Fluffy Pants said
'You're old and bald
And you have a wrinkly head!'

The Queen got angry
And called the Royal Navy.
As soon as they arrived,
He splatted them with cook's finest gravy.

She ordered them to drown him.
But it didn't seem to work
He pulled himself onto the bank
And stole a big, white Merc.

He found a time machine
And went back to this morning
To the time he was still sleeping
And he woke up still snoring.

Spongebob Fluffy Pants lives in the air
in a cardboard box
Putting on his fluffy pants
and his old woollen socks.

Daniel Siner & Jack Howes (10)
Auriol Junior School, Epsom

War Of The Monsters

Monster Land was a land of peace . . . once.
But then other monsters came, they had weapons and fur all over.
They were bad and made us really sad.
They started in the A zone and got to our throne.
They took over Monster Land or so they thought.
Another monster came and he fought.
He had a fist as hard as stone and his pincer
could crush your skull like a can!
His third arm had a gun that fired slime!
The enemy was running out of time
They waited until night, then he came to fight
He pushed his way to their leader, he acted as if he was The Slender
They blinked, he got closer, his third arm secretly came out of his back
Then they both shouted 'Attack!'
A while passed, there was nothing but devastation.
He wanted no attention.
He had saved Monster Land.
Then he left . . .

James Wheeler (10)
Auriol Junior School, Epsom

Piranha Man

Who do you know that has a bowl on his head
Who eats things like humans in a stress,
He is a cannibal eater,
And sleeps in a mess,
Nobody knows who he is or where he goes,
Only the people who have witnessed his toes,
Piranha man who takes over the world,
Big and scary everybody knows,
You can feel his presence wherever he goes,
Big and tall and full of fire,
Sparking off a terrible desire,
To get rid of human power,
And start a race with monster power.

Shaun Silverside (10)
Auriol Junior School, Epsom

A Day Out With A Monster

My monster comes from a different planet,
He left everyone, even his mum called Janet.
My monster doesn't have any food,
even though he is in a good mood.
We went to the Eiffel Tower,
I brought my monster a flower.
We had lunch and I brought him everything there,
and he left a tip, just one hair.
My monster had to go back now,
Just before he left I got him a cow.
He went back home to his planet,
and all that time the monster was Janet.

Oliver Brown (11)
Auriol Junior School, Epsom

Monster Crime

Have you seen a crime,
But not as big as a monster?
Well this monster likes crime.
He fights like a lion, and makes a crime without a pint,
Have you seen a monster make a crime without a rhyme?
Have you seen a monster make a crime without a might?
Have you seen a monster make a crime without a try?
Have you seen a monster make a crime without a prize?

Kloe Brahimi (10)
Auriol Junior School, Epsom

Blob And Me . . .

Monday: time to take the laundry.
Come on Blob, time to go.
Blob where are you?
Seriously, hiding in the laundry basket!

Tuesday: Why don't we go to an Antique shop?
Don't touch anything Blob, stop!
You're going to drop that casket!

Wednesday: Let's go and watch a show.
Please don't go and dance on stage.
Blob noooo!

Thursday: Why don't we stay at home.
It's not going to harm us.
Stop! Silly Blob you're covered in huss!

Friday: come on, let's go shopping . . . never again!

Grace Giangregorio (11)
Auriol Junior School, Epsom

My Monster

This is a poem about a monster so small,
Not evil or slimy or scary at all, but
He's tiny, naughty, nice, devious and cool
He likes making mischief and being a ball
He's fluffy and his name's Jeff
He likes causing me stress
He bounces around the room
So high he touches the moon, noisy, hairy, nice, that's my monster
He loves yummy snacks, they're bigger than him,
He loves the water but he can't swim.
His moustache is so fluffy and cute
To parties he wears a fur suit
He'll eat anything especially soup
Now it's time for bed, say bye to your friend
Even though he stays up on YouTube and Minecraft instead
Don't stay away come and play
With Jeff Jefferson my friend.

Poppy Moore (11)
Auriol Junior School, Epsom

Trip To The Queen's Palace

Rickson was a giant,
Fat, ugly, but happy monster.
Rickson went on a trip
To see the Queen,
He met the Queen,
To have a meet and greet,
And had a tour of the palace.
It was very poor.

Rickson was hungry
So he went on a search to find some meat
'Cause Rickson wanted a teat.
He found a piece of meat
And decided to eat the meat.
It was hairy like a lion. 'Yummy!'

Alyssa Chaiprakhom (11)
Auriol Junior School, Epsom

War Of The Monsters

Monsterland was a land of peace . . . once
But then other monsters came, they had weapons and fur all over.
They were bad and made us really sad.
They started in the A zone and got to our throne.
They took over Monsterland or so they thought.
Another monster came and he fought.
He had a fist as hard as stone and his pincer could crush your skull like a can!
His third arm had a gun that fired slime.
The enemy was running out of time.
They waited until night, then he came to fight.
He pushed his way to their leader, he acted as if he was The Slender
They blinked, he got closer, his third arm secretly came out of his back.
Then they both shouted 'Attack!'
A while passed, there was nothing but devastation.
He wanted no attention.
He had saved Monsterland.
Then he left . . .

Oliver Pearce (10)
Auriol Junior School, Epsom

Death Dude!

There is a giant monster
Somewhere near the Indian sea.
It is as fat and furry
And as scary as can be.

Its claws are sharp and spiky
And its eyes are crimson red.

Were it to jump up ten miles high
and fell down with a *boom*
The whole Earth would then shake
We'd think we are at doom.

Dean Kerrins (10)
Auriol Junior School, Epsom

It's Like A Beast

It's like a beast
That comes at night
The children hide
It gives them a fright.

It's like a beast
It's freaky and fierce
It spooks all the kids
Especially Pierce.

It's like a beast
Its teeth are like knives
They're dangerous like razors
They kill lives.

It's like a beast
That comes at night
It will return
It might, it might . . .

Caleb Heather (11)
Auriol Junior School, Epsom

Ozzy Saves The Day

Ozzy was at a football match,
Then he hatched an egg,
And suddenly, an evil alien came down,
He had a frown,
Why oh why was he here?
He was here to ruin the match.
So Ozzy jumped down,
And breaks the frown off his brown face,
And then the evil alien becomes best friends with Ozzy,
Now the evil alien is a good alien,
He lives with us now,
We even gave him a new name,
His is called Spike.

Gemma Lambert (10)
Auriol Junior School, Epsom

Fred

My monster Fred is the coolest thing ever
He's green
He's slimy
And he wears a jacket that's leather

One day Fred and I went to a theme park
With a loop the loop and the sound of screaming and yelling
Our feet never touched the ground!

By lunchtime
He wasn't the monster he seemed to be
He got very hungry -
That was the end of me!

Imogen Malone (10)
Auriol Junior School, Epsom

Me And My Monster

I have a monster called Fred,
He lives just here under my bed,
In the middle of the night,
He gave me a fright,
So I hit him on the head,
He looked so sad,
And I felt so bad,
That in the end,
He became my best friend,
One day we went to the shop,
He got hungry and ate a mop,
But still he felt hungry,
So ate a little girl's toy monkey,
Her mum told the shop boss,
And she got very cross,
She was less than pleased,
And asked us to leave,
We had to go home,
When I got home Fred had eaten my phone!

Daisie Fletcher (10)
Auriol Junior School, Epsom

My Monster

My monster has got a runny nose,
And she makes a funny pose,
When she sneezes in her claws.

I hope she gets well soon,
Because she wants to travel to the moon,
And swim in a cheesy pool.

Sabina Kecha (10)
Auriol Junior School, Epsom

Don't Look Down

This is it, the way to doom
Dread fills me up
'I can do this'
Then suddenly he
Looked down.

Once he looked down
He got the fright
Of his life
He saw a monster with eight eyes.

When he finally got to know the monster,
They became best friends.

Josh Banyard (11)
Auriol Junior School, Epsom

My Pet Monster

My pet monster
Went in the washing machine,
He spun round and round
My monster was clean.

My pet monster
He was now very naughty
My monster painted on the walls
He even broke my trampoline.

My pet monster
Who loved to make mischief,
he kicked a ball at a window,
How naughty could he be.

Lucy Taylor (11)
Auriol Junior School, Epsom

My Friend Kittycat

I've got a friend called
KittyCat and she loves
Eating Kitkats and
Absolutely likes Tictacs.
And she likes to box,
So don't go near her
Because, she'll make you flop.
Give her all you've got,
Otherwise, she'll make you drop.
So let's go out and buy some crops
In the shops.

Elena Keshvadi (10)
Auriol Junior School, Epsom

Mike

Hey my name is Mike,
I've got a friend, his name is Sully,
He's blue and purple and has green eyes.

I'm green with blue eyes,
Me and Sully are besties,
We stay in a room together.

My favourite food is cupcakes,
I love my girlfriend Selia,
I love her so much.

Please have a good day.

Molly Howard-Lawrence (11)
Auriol Junior School, Epsom

My Little Monster And Me

Its eyes are small
Yet he seems tall
My little monster and me.

His cuteness scares
He will raise all your hairs
My little monster and me.

He's so sneaky
It is freaky
My little monster and me.

He jumps out at night
And will give you a fright
My little monster and me.

We had lots of fun
And now our day's done
My little monster and me.

Jessica Elliott (10)
Auriol Junior School, Epsom

Da Blob Takes Over The World

I know a monster who wants to take over the world,
He has been planning for a while.

He eats gloopy jelly with glowing bread
And has disgusting warts on the top of his head.

He can transform into anything a car, a plane, a train or a boat.
Or maybe he might be your winter coat.

He can hypnotise you with a blink of his eye
And can read minds when he looks at your backside.

He is gargantuan with four beady red eyes and six wiggly arms.
He hates humans because they think they are so clever.

I have seen him fly by in his UFO.
When I saw him I thought to myself, 'Oh no.'

Maybe one day he will attempt to take over the world
But I assure you he will probably fail
Well at least I hope so.

Pierce Hopkins (11)
Auriol Junior School, Epsom

A Day Out To Nursery

Me and Moni Bob
Went to a nursery
First we went to class 3P
All those people were making a plastic tree
We scared a person called Freddie.

Next we went to 4D
How old could they be?
They were learning about a cat's paw
We scared a Russian person called Yardin Gore

Next we went to 5S
That was a class that no one liked
But no one would ever confess
Then we went home and had a nice, big rest.

Billy Tarbuck (10)
Auriol Junior School, Epsom

Frank Takes Over The World

Once I had a monster,
His name was Frank,
And he always broke the bank,
His aim was to take over the world,
But his bullets always curled,
First he took over Paris,
And then bought a Honda Yaris,
He took over the USA,
And then played with clay,
Then he took over the world
And his bullets never curled.

Adam Stubbs (12)
Auriol Junior School, Epsom

The Day My Monster Met The King

My monster had a pet lobster
He was fuzzy and furry
And was very, very hairy.

He had cute little eyes
And loves to eat rice
He's orange and adorable
But at night he's abominable.

Ferocious and speedy
His eyes become beady
Now he has razor sharp teeth
And at night his favourite food is actually beef.

One day my monster was invited to have tea with the King!
When I got there my monster was tucked into a chicken wing.
When it was dark,
The King was gone, in the time a dog could bark.

That was the day my monster met the King.

David Kelly (11)
Auriol Junior School, Epsom

Untitled

There is a monster in my cupboard,
I'm not sure what to do.
There's a monster under my bed
And a monster in my shoe.

One has green hair
Down to his knees.
Another one likes to
Cough and sneeze!

We are monsters,
Creatures at night.
We have arrived,
To bring you a fright!

Daniel Goncalves (11)
Auriol Junior School, Epsom

Evian, The Hero Of The Day

One day there was a monster called Evian
He was very harmless but he could eat you
And he had lots of friends
He was fat, funny, he had a big mouth.
There was a bad guy in the town
And he put a bomb in the town
They did not know what to do
They were all scared that it would go off
Until Evian wanted to do something
So he ate the bomb and it stopped
He was the hero of the day

Ethan Winter (11)
Auriol Junior School, Epsom

Blue Blobby

I have got a monster friend called Blobby
Skipping is his favourite hobby
He has one eye and his colour is blue
At the end of his hand he has fingers, two.
To look at him he is very gooey,
If you ate him, he would probably be chewy.

One night we went out to eat
Blobby wanted an extra treat
I got him an ice cream
On the television he watched the football team.

When we went home
Blobby got out his phone
We had a night that was fun
Me and my monster chum.

Emily Attewell (10)
Auriol Junior School, Epsom

My Massive Monster

One day I found a monster,
We went to see a pop star,
He is from Zog,
Which is a huge log,
All they eat is yum yums,
Now they have big tum tums,
I named him Tangs,
Because of his fangs,
I bought him some Tangfastics,
He thought they were fantastic,
I said goodbye,
Then started to cry,
I then woke up and said sup to my mum,
Who said I'd been asleep for ages!

Pranav Ganesh (11)
Auriol Junior School, Epsom

The Monster Saved My Life!

In the deep, dark room
I heard someone in the room,
And I was scared
But I was brave enough
To go in the deep, dark room,
I couldn't see but I felt a hairy little creature
Suddenly I fell down a little crack on the floor,
But I was saved by the monster
And we made friends.
Then my little monster, who was called Libey,
Came over to my house for tea,
And we had roast for tea,
Then a cake for pudding,
But I was not too sure if she did like cake,
Then I found out,
Slowly that two cakes were missing,
So I asked if anyone had seen my cakes
That were missing,
But no one had a cake so,
I looked around the house
But still found nothing
Suddenly I spotted pink fur on the plate
So I asked Libey because she had pink fur
And it was her
So of course she loved cakes!

Tia Le Page (10)
Auriol Junior School, Epsom

Armageddon Catches A Robber

Armageddon is not your typical scary monster
His young owner Chris had a friend called Ronnie (or Ronster!)
But this is the tale of when Armageddon saved the day.

It started with him and Chris sometime in May
The TV came on and they began to watch.
Then Chris' dad came in holding a scotch.
'What are we watching then?' dad said.
'I'm hungry,' Armageddon said and went out to get some bread,
As we got there Armageddon 20/20 vision looked at all the vibrant shops
Then we saw some cops, chasing a clown.
At first Armageddon thought it was funny, but then stated, 'This is no stunt!'
With an amazing jump off the moving stair, he grabbed the clown and pulled him down.
He was the best monster ever, they said
And Armageddon was so happy,
He felt as light as a feather.

Christopher Sargent (11)
Auriol Junior School, Epsom

John The Growly Monster

John the monster
Was very growly.
He had great big green, cheesy feet.
He had big sharp nails
To catch snails.

Charlie Foreman (10)
Auriol Junior School, Epsom

Hairball

My monster's name is Hairball,
He's really big and scary,
He's not allowed to go to school,
Because he's blue and hairy.
My monster came from Pluto, travelling on a ray of light,
He looked just like a moonbeam,
A streak of bright light out of sight.
My monster is very deadly,
Basically not friendly,
He hasn't washed for at least a month
And every time he itches, he makes a sound like 'Unth.'
My monster is very tall and has a big favourite ball.
He is always up for a fight
And he'll give you an awful big fright!

Isabel Lynton-Jenkins (10)
Auriol Junior School, Epsom

The Monster Teacher

My monster is blue just like you,
He's ultra rare!
He has a friend like a teddy bear
Who likes a pear a day.
But they both just don't pay.

He has five eyes that don't tell lies,
He has one ear that helps him drink beer!

He has done a great honour
To help his old class teacher teach the young ones
How to control their anger
By playing teacher's lair all day.

Morgan (10)
Auriol Junior School, Epsom

Trevor

This monster is called Trevor
He's the scariest monster ever!
He has ten eyes and can see very well,
He has three noses and has a great sense of smell!
If you see him please try and hide,
Otherwise he'll be right by your side!
He eats everything for dinner
Especially animals and people.
He won't get any thinner!
His skin is scaly and shiny,
And his claws are sharp and slimy!

Alex Chambers (10)
Auriol Junior School, Epsom

The Monster's Journey

On a bright, breezy, brilliant day
A monster was on a journey to anywhere,
Anywhere but home.
She travels by flying in the air.
A day passed, she found a beautiful big town
But behind the beautiful, big town,
Was a grand, gigantic gatehouse to a castle.
But a big blazing fire she could see.
The King and Queen were exquisite, but yet no princess.
Underground a terrible tyrant terrified the trembling people.
Yet the fire got higher than a pyre.
The princess was fair and her name was Claire.
The monster saved her with her long dangly hair
From the monster called Dare.

Hadley Rose (10)
Auriol Junior School, Epsom

My Monster From Emerald Star

My monster, Lydia, from Emerald Star,
Travelled to Earth from her planet afar.
She was dangerous, ferocious, but made of fluff,
She looked soft and cuddly, but was oh so tough.

Her mission on Earth was to find Emerald stones,
She searched the rocks but found dinosaur bones.
She looked in lakes, rivers and the sea,
She stopped at times to eat some tea.

Finally, one day, she had some luck,
She saw a green glisten on a Mallard duck.
She realised the emeralds were in the pond,
She pulled from her pocket, a magical wand.

With a swash and a swish,
She produced a dish.
She collected gems green,
And vanished from the scene.

My monster Lydia from Emerald Star,
Had travelled back home to her planet afar.

Abigail Harris (10)
Auriol Junior School, Epsom

My TV Monster

He came out of the TV
And went to the park,
He jumped out of his pants when he heard a dog bark.
We made a tent out of sticks and stones,
My mum said, 'Be careful, you might break your bones.'

Harvey Tilbury (10)
Auriol Junior School, Epsom

Creepy Charlie's Adventure

Creepy Charlie is from a forest
He lives with his brother, his name is Boris
Boris is not Charlie's friend
Boris drives him round the bend
Creepy Charlie is very glum
As he does not have a chum
He knows he is good and very kind
Sadly a friend he cannot find
Creepy Charlie is black with red spots
His favourite dinner is lamb chops
One day he met a girl called Nieve
By mistake he chewed her sleeve
The monster's face became very sad
As he realised he had been bad
'Please don't cry,' said Nieve, 'I will be your friend.
I have thread, my sleeve I can mend.'
The day was over, they made plans to meet
Chessington World of Adventures, oh what a treat.

Nieve Penford (10)
Auriol Junior School, Epsom

When My Monster Came To Tea

My monster is from a different planet
He has a mum called Janet
When my monster came to tea
I took him for lunch with the Queen
The Queen said he was green,
And looked very mean.
But she liked him all the same
And asked him if he would like his monster main.
My monster's name is Spikey
And he is very slimy.
'Your name is nice,' said the Queen
'Oh and don't you look clean,'
And they finished their day with pie
After going on the London Eye.

Holly Osbond (10)
Auriol Junior School, Epsom

Days Out With My Monster

A day out with my monster
Up in my rocket
We landed on the moon
And he grabbed onto my pocket.

A day out with my monster
Along the seaside
We were having a lot of fun,
Until he ran to hide.

A day out with my monster
Climbing all the trees
Swinging on the branches
He fell and hurt his knees.

Days out with my monster
They are all so fun
After using all that energy
I think I need a bun.

Joanna Loosley (10)
Auriol Junior School, Epsom

My Very Special Monster

Monsters are big, monsters are small,
But my monster is very tall,
My monster isn't a fool, but she is very cool,
She has big feet and little toes,
She really doesn't know that she has a miniature nose,
But she's my monster and I love her,
Even though she has long fur.

Leoni Stewart (10)
Auriol Junior School, Epsom

Me And My Monster Brian

My monster he's my awesome pet
He looks big and scary
The best monster I've ever met
He's awfully hairy
His name is Brian
He's so gentle
He roars like a lion
My mum goes mental
One day we went to space
In Brian's shiny, red rocket
He had such a happy face
In space I found a golden locket!
We came home for ice cream
Then we went to the beach
Our day was supreme
My ice cream flavour was peach
My monster Brian he's my awsome pet.

Areezah (10)
Auriol Junior School, Epsom

A Day Out With Joe!

Meet Joe, he lives under a bridge in Soho
Joe doesn't have any real friends, his only friend is his teddy Leo.
He is gooey old Joe, and sticks to everything in his sight.
It gives the locals a fright.
He goes to the funfair on his own
And goes on the rides.
Joe's always tried to find friends at the funfair
But they always run away,
Poor old Joe got a tiny soul,
So that is Joe, he is a poor old soul
And maybe, just maybe, he might find a friend in Soho!

Phoebe Wilton (10)
Auriol Junior School, Epsom

Philip

'What's that, coming over the hill?'
'It's a monster,
'Is it a monster?'
'What's that, coming over the hill?
Is it a monster?'
'It's my pet monster.'
I sit down and do my homework,
I sometimes fart,
I let it rip,
Then my monster pops up to help me,
His name is Philip,
He helps me lots,
He is my friend,
He also drives me round the bend, right round the bend!

Tommie Culver (11)
Auriol Junior School, Epsom

The Monster

My monster is black, hairy and tall
And has red spots
And is 100ft tall.
He has nine heads which have fifty teeth,
And his feet are as long as a hall,
And also his name is Paul.

Sean Murphy (11)
Auriol Junior School, Epsom

My Monster, Matcombe

My monster comes from planet Mars
And likes to eat chocolate bars.
I am his best ever mate,
When he eats, he needs more than one plate,
He is a bad monster, but good to me,
Although he is very stinky.
I would go to Spain,
But we would need to get a massive plane.
If we did we would play in the sea,
And he would be really happy.

Charlie Knott (10)
Auriol Junior School, Epsom

Spooky Tale

There was a monster, he was vicious
And sometimes he could be very suspicious.
He was afraid of going home
Because when he got there,
His mum would moan.
He left home feeling sad,
He decided if no one likes him
He might as well be bad.

Ronnie Andrews (10)
Auriol Junior School, Epsom

Scary Cave Dave

There once was a monster who lived in a cave,
He was ever so scary, for a name called Dave.
He had purple pricks all over his back,
He was hairy all over and his teeth were jet black,
He was always trying to find a friend,
And on the lonely nights he'd spend,
Time thinking on what it would be like to have a friend.
He would dream and dream every night,
Then he woke up with such a fright,
With a monster who looked like him with purple pricks all over his back
And was hairy all over and teeth jet black
Then he said, his name was Tim.

Jacob Griffin (11)
Auriol Junior School, Epsom

My Monster Dinner Man

Today we got stew that you have to chew
And juice that smells like a baby's loo.

Tuesday we got tongue of dog and slime of frog.

Wednesday we got head of cat and blood of bat.

Thursday we got mud pie and a weird potion
That can make you die.

Frida we got nothing, so now we are really starving.

And that's the dinner man we'd be better off
Having a plain old tin can.

Krista Abbott (10)
Auriol Junior School, Epsom

When I Met Tiny

My monster friend, my awesome pet
She jumped in a pond and got very wet
On Mars there are no cars,
That's why we never met.

My monster is called Tiny
She never makes a mess
I have never known her to be whiney
She is as pink as my new pink dress.

I said I'd visit her home one day
That I would go around to play.
But my parents wouldn't let me go away
So here I will have to stay.

Amelia Boardman (11)
Auriol Junior School, Epsom

The Monster On The Moon

I met a monster in an alleyway,
He was black and blue,
I went up to him,
And he looked seven foot two.
I said, 'What do you want to do?'
He said, 'I wanna fly to the moon!'
I said, 'Fine, I've got a rocket!
We can fly just me and you!'
They finally arrived on the moon,
Jackow asked for his name,
The monster replied, 'Bob.'
And Jackow replied, 'OK.'
They saw a spot and sat down,
The whole world could see their shadow,
As dark as the midnight light,
The Monster said, 'I'll miss you, young old Jackow!'

Seif Kalatch (10)
Beulah Junior School, Thornton Heath

Erblubba

Erblubba the blind,
Can't see what he finds.

He is three feet tall,
With no limbs at all.

He's got slime all over his black and white tie,
He is immortal so he'll never die.

Born in an accident - the chemical kind,
But doesn't know that I think you will find.

Spotblubby's his friend, and so is Dan Blub,
And that's not forgetting Plub, Wib and Falub.

Smifflub's the dim one, he can't fix a blister,
Sidlub and Toob are brother and sister.

They live in our world and go to Blob Street School,
Their teacher is kind and called Mr Pool.

Remember Erblubba can't see,
It sounds like a problem to me.

He can't find the school entrance gate,
So every morning he's too late.

You see? Erblubba doesn't.

His palour is perfect purple,
His hopper is ormented orange.

His glasses are as round as a full moon,
His smile is as cute as a minion.

His catablob fires slimy slugs,
His head is as squidgy as trifle.

He's not a friendly monster,
He's one of the menacing kind.

His pillow is filled with solid goo,
His place in class is at the front.

You see? Erblubba doesn't.

William Smith (9)
Beulah Junior School, Thornton Heath

Heath Burns

I met a monster,
In a playground
He had fire hair
And a named tattoo
You needed gloves to touch him.

He was a bit shy,
And almost cried
But he was fine.
Heath explained
Where he was from
Planet Kripton was its name.

We played around
Screamed and shouted,
His planet was creepy, crazy and funny.

Heath asked for a deal,
I said, 'How about a meal?'
No two things of mine and yours
Much much more to explore.

The way we played his monster games
Were like wind blowing me away;
We went to his planet but needed goggles to see it.

One day we played my games
We realised we were sort of the same.
Heath had to go home
But promised to visit again.

Rhianna (9)
Beulah Junior School, Thornton Heath

Forest-Fires' Last Adventure

One clear night,
I had the most thrilling adventure of my life,
There was a shooting star dancing across the night,
Oh the comet that night.

I was led to a beach where it had grown rather tiny,
Guess what it had set the sand alight,
'Hello my name is Spark, and I'm going to a special place this night,'
Oh the comet that night.

So I went to a lab,
That looked rather dull,
Zap bang zap night,
Oh the comet that night.

A scientist whisked it away,
As soon as it turned into a fireball,
Its name was Fires and came out at night,
Oh the comet that night.

A machine whirred in far corner of the room,
Two tanks gleamed in the light,
It began in the middle of the night,
Oh the comet that night.

The spark lived in the lab,
The monster lived in Mount Everest,
Oh that comet that clear night.

Kristen (9)
Beulah Junior School, Thornton Heath

My Sweet Monster Friend

As I strolled to my school gate,
A beam flashed down from the sky.
Out came a little furry monster,
Who looked very polite!
I introduced myself, while leading her inside
My teacher stroked the adorable little creature,
After saying her cute name.
'Shelly is my name'
It finally came to lunchtime,
I had my pack-lunch ready.
With a *zap* and a *zoom*
A pink-with-yellow-striped cotton candy
Appeared in Shelly's hand.
Then with a *whoosh* it disappeared,
Never seen again.
The end of school came shortly, everyone leaving.
Shelly waved goodbye and slowly faded away.

Deveen Carnegie (10)
Beulah Junior School, Thornton Heath

The Monster

A monster called this morning,
He came in the light of day,
A monster called this morning and whisked me away.
At first we walked down the road
Then ran at the speed of sound,
Then when we came to a halt I found . . .
A whole group of monsters as far as the eye could see.
A whole group of monsters and they asked me to tea.
I stared at the table, there was so much to eat,
There was cake and biscuits and a lot of meat.
Then when we finished eating I went home,
Then my monster left and I was alone.

Oluoma Onugha (10)
Beulah Junior School, Thornton Heath

That Monster Danger

When I went out with my dad
That day, it sure was a big surprise.
My dad threw the ball, as I sat on a stool,
And I ran for the ball at sunrise.
I ran for the ball and thought I might fall.

As I sat on a rock, still alive,
I turned around, stunned at what I saw.
He was really poor,
Also ten foot tall.
He was as tall as a twenty brick wall.

He asked me to eat me
I said 'Oh yes'
I was being sarcastic.
But he said 'Oh bless'
He was perilous and proud,
He was notorious and nasty.
He bit my butt,
He put me in his mouth and gobbled me up!

Victor Jibuike (9)
Beulah Junior School, Thornton Heath

Will Wants A Life Of His Own

He has a friend called Dil.
Dil was the best friend in the world
They played outside,
And knocked for Millie.
There was a robber stealing from the bank.
They caught the robber,
And called the police.
They are the hero monsters.

Sean Smith (8)
Dewhurst St Mary CE Primary School, Waltham Cross

Daisy Adventure

Once a fluffy monster came to a shop.
I asked what her name was.
Her name was Daisy.
She was multicoloured.
Daisy always ran swiftly.
Daisy saw people stealing things.
She ran quickly and she got the burglars.

Meryem Tutuman (8)
Dewhurst St Mary CE Primary School, Waltham Cross

Monster Cat

The colourful monster cat,
Saw a tiny, black hat.
It was placed on the fluffy, red mat,
And next to it was his friend Pat.
Pat said 'What is that?'
I replied, 'It's a monster cat.'
Suddenly . . . appeared a bat,
It swooped down and stole the tiny black hat,
Up jumped the cat,
Grabbing the tiny, black hat
From the claws of the evil bat.
The cat got the hat,
It was torn to pieces by the bat,
And that was the end of the tiny, black hat.

Stevie Cotterell (7)
Dewhurst St Mary CE Primary School, Waltham Cross

Mr Droolsaloot's Big Day

On Tuesday I met a monster
I brought him to my house
He said 'Have you got any venom?'
We played in my room
He was called Droolsaloot,
Then we went in my bunk bed
The next day we went to school
He ate my lunch
Then we did it all over again,
I woke up and Droolsaloot had to do a mission
He had to go to his planet,
I never saw him again.

Freddie Coats (8)
Dewhurst St Mary CE Primary School, Waltham Cross

Super Monster

In the forest there was a monster
Who frightened the evil emperor lobster.
Lucky Colour was his name
His colours were not lame.
He took me into space
It was a crazy time race.
We saved the universe together
After that he gave me a piece of leather
It was a time watch
Which was top notch.
I could travel anywhere
Would people stop and stare?
A new adventure to have each day
For now I'm off to play.

Louis Ahmet (7)
Dewhurst St Mary CE Primary School, Waltham Cross

The Honey Suckle Monster

One day at school,
I met a monster,
Called Honey Suckle.
She liked flying in the sky,
And lived in the ocean.
We took off and flew to her home.
Underwater we saw,
Lots of fish multicoloured,
And all shapes and sizes.
We slept in her bed that night
And in the morning we flew back to school
Just in time.

Evie McGarry (8)
Dewhurst St Mary CE Primary School, Waltham Cross

The Mean Monster

We went to the market
I saw a colourful, spiky monster.
He had four eyes and looked mean.
He ate all the yellow bananas.
He was running and said goodbye.
The CCTV saw him eat all the yellow bananas.
Then the police saw him and he ran out of the market.
Then he ran in a giant pocket.
The police went in the park and looked.
The monster went out of the giant pocket
He pushed the police in the pond.
He stole a magical wand.
He changed the shop into his gigantic house.
He made with his wand some household.
He made a fridge, freezer, oven and sofa.
He even made a washing machine, computer and television.

Wiktor Kolenda (7)
Dewhurst St Mary CE Primary School, Waltham Cross

The Trip To The Beach

Walking down to the beach,
I heard a tiny voice say,
'Would you like to play with me?'
'I'd love to,' I replied.
Off we went.
We saw a castle and smelt a BBQ.
It made us hungry.
Some people let us have some of their food.
The hot dogs were delicious,
And we were having so much fun.
That she melted because it was very hot.
My monster was made of ice cream.

Darcy Wilson (3)
Dewhurst St Mary CE Primary School, Waltham Cross

The Orange, Blue And Green Monster

Monster, monster, under my bed,
Help, help, it has ten heads.
He's blue, orange and green,
He's very keen on being mean.
Roary is mad
He makes everyone sad.
Roary is loud,
He's the only sound around!
Roary is vile,
He really has no style.
He never cries or else he will die,
And he's very, very, very sly.

Rebecca Mansford (7)
Dewhurst St Mary CE Primary School, Waltham Cross

The One Eyed Monster

Once there was a giant monster,
I saw him in the woods one day,
He lurks in the shadows at night,
He comes from a volcano with lava,
He eats dead animals and sucks blood,
And he always spies on people,
He is very mean and evil,
He had legs like an octopus,
His ears are like bees antennas,
His eye is round like a balloon,
He caught a boy one day,
He was never ever seen again . . .

Grace McGarry (7)
Dewhurst St Mary CE Primary School, Waltham Cross

Googlie's Amazing Adventure

One day when I went to school,
I saw a orange monster.
It's name is Googlie.
His dream was to be a clown,
In a town.
We went to the funfair,
And we saw a big grizzle bear.
He smelt delicious candyfloss
I spotted beautiful lipgloss.
Today is our last day,
As he goes back to Sillyworld in May.

Naomi Latinwo (7)
Dewhurst St Mary CE Primary School, Waltham Cross

Squiggles Goes To Space

Walking down my town one day,
I heard a little monster say,
'My name is Squiggles,
I'm as purple as pickles.
But if you help me,
I'll do what you say.
I need to fly in every way,
Where no one else can ever play.
I'm very tired,
So you're not fired.
Help me with this right now,
Before you go tumbling down.
So this is it,
I've got no lists,
Because we are out of this.
So I am going,
But I'll be sewing.
So bye.
And off you fly.
I'll be your friend forever.
And thank you for the new colour leather.'

Samantha Gold (7)
Dewhurst St Mary CE Primary School, Waltham Cross

I'm Into Space

I'm in the rocket for long enough
Even though it's very rough
I've just taken off and saw Santa
Eating biscuits and drinking Fanta
I flew over a school
Which looked gorgeous and cool
It was enormous and pink
And a student gave me a wink
I've landed on Earth
Just in time to see Mummy give birth
I am walking around
To find a friend
I saw a dog which jumped on me
Who had lots of fleas
So I brushed his fur
He said to me 'Mur'
And oh no it's time to go
I have to say my name is Freindla
And I might come another day.

Aleksandra Kolenda (7)
Dewhurst St Mary CE Primary School, Waltham Cross

Horns The Mean Monster

One day I was eating food
Then went outside.
Then I saw a big shadow,
It was a monster.
It has a name not sure,
But didn't have money, so he's poor.
His name is Horns,
He is crazy so be careful.
That monster is crawly,
And is very drooly.
But then he went home,
Under his little dome.

Lewis Okekumata (7)
Dewhurst St Mary CE Primary School, Waltham Cross

Three Eyes

Walking in the park on a sunny day,
I met a monster, called Three Eyes on the way.
His body was blue and his face was green.
He was tall and lean.
This monster is really shy,
Suddenly, he started to cry.
He was crying because I left him
And then I told him my name was Kim.
We played on the swings and the slide
Then we had a ride
He has three eyes and they are white
Three Eyes saw a light, but it was not real.
He disappeared in a flash, I did not know how to feel.
My day had been strange, but fun,
I couldn't believe everything I d done.

Sydney Knight (7)
Dewhurst St Mary CE Primary School, Waltham Cross

Slimy's Fun Adventure

'Come and play ball with me
'Can I yes thank you yes please.'
Slimy came round my house tonight for tea
Next time we can go in the sea.
I love your silky skin
And you're really thin.
I can smell the BBQ
And I'm reading a book, and I'm halfway through.
We can go to the park,
We can go with Mark.
I think his doorbell is loud,
I'm very proud.
'To get home do you want to go in my car?'
'Yes because my house is really far!'

Holly-Mai Gaskin (7)
Dewhurst St Mary CE Primary School, Waltham Cross

Caramel's Trip To School

Turning round the corner was a cheery monster.
Skipping to school saying 'I am in Year 1.'
He heard a clever mouse talking.
'Oh where oh where are my school clothes?'
'Hello little ballet mouse, what's wrong?'
'I've lost my clothes.'
'No you haven't, you're wearing them.'
'Thank you,' said the little mouse
So little monster set off for school.
My school is so big I am scared.
There were lots of paper in Class 1.
'I should pick it up' he said.
'You're doing the right thing' said Miss Appleberry.
The children's names were Strawberry, Blueberry, Kiwi, Orange and Banana.
'Hometime,' shouted Miss Appleberry. 'I am proud of you.
Don't forget to do your homework.'
The mouse said, 'Thank you,' and flew home . . .

Ellia Perone (7)
Dewhurst St Mary CE Primary School, Waltham Cross

Rock Star Monster

Why can't I have a monster?
But they're not real
I can try and make one in the lab
What do I need?
Let me ask a friend to help me
I know I'll ask the lab robot Sam
'Sam can you help me?'
I have a spell book
I can get it by magic
Now I will make a rock star monster
Da da honky tonk la la la.

Sonny Grant (8)
Great Ballard School, Chichester

Monster

I was walking on the street
I saw a bloodthirsty monster
He was a very big monster
He had three heads, one hundred and six legs, eighty three arms and no body!
In one of his hands there was a . . . a . . . minute monster
With a polka dot bikini
'Let me go'
The monster dropped him and he fell asleep.

Sam Thomas (7)
Great Ballard School, Chichester

The Putty Monster

One day I made a putty monster
His name was Zinc
I left him in the kitchen all night
That night he came to life
In the morning . . .
I rushed downstairs to the kitchen
When I opened the door
There was an . . . humongous monster!

Oscar Young (7)
Great Ballard School, Chichester

Night Monster

When it was night I was asleep
I woke because I'd heard a noise
I could smell it and it seemed friendly
I saw it and it was fluffy
It was silky.

Freya Dowdall (7)
Great Ballard School, Chichester

Monster

My monster is a nice monster, happy monster, helpful monster.
A musical monster, spotty monster, fluffy monster, funny monster.
Most of all a loveable monster.
A noisy monster, fit monster, hairy monster, cool monster.
Small monster, rockstar monster, pretty monster, soft monster.
I love my monster, and he loves me.
Remember all monsters are loveable, he lives with me in my own little house in England.

Emma Curry (7)
Great Ballard School, Chichester

Horrible Monsters

I closed the door and went to sleep.
I was in a horrible nightmare I was dreaming monsters.
The monsters were very big and spotty,
Each day he came and ate my dinner!

Claudio Schuetz (7)
Great Ballard School, Chichester

The Monsters Who Went To Tea

There were two small monsters
That came to tea with me
There was one large green monster
That came to tea with me
There were three teeny purple monsters
That came to tea with me
We ate and ate until we popped!

Billy English (7)
Great Ballard School, Chichester

Uh Oh

In the middle of the night
I felt something crawling up my bed.
It felt slimy, sticky, spiky and hairy!
I took off the covers
I saw a horrible sight . . . !
It was a scary looking dog.
I checked if there were any more
I thought where did it come from?
When I opened my bedroom door there were lots of monsters.
Aaaaaargh!

Bevan Morrison (7)
Great Ballard School, Chichester

The Monster In The Woods

A scary monster in a tree
'Come to the woods,' he said
Then the child saw the monster
'You are skinny,' he said
The monster ran to its mummy
'I am so scared,' he said
But the child just wanted to be his friend.

Archie Lovelock (7)
Great Ballard School, Chichester

The Monster In The Night

One night,
I had a fright,
I heard a noise under my bed,
I sat up quickly and turned my head,
I saw a monster on the floor,
It looked a lot like a boar,
He made me stay up 'til after dawn,
Then I did a drowsy yawn,
He finally said,
'Let's get to bed.'
The next morning I looked under my bed,
But all I saw was my dragon's head,
He never came to my bed once more,
Probably 'cause I really snore!

Luke Griffiths (10)
High View Primary School, Wallington

The Silly Monster

As I was walking to school the bush was shaking,
So I carefully walked over to the bush although I was feeling a little bit scared,
When I got there it was a monster, he had a bumpy banana on his red and slimy head.
He went with me to school, he was allowed to come in, but he dashed into the classroom,
He tipped the water bottles into the bin, it was obvious he had never been in a classroom before,
So I took him outside before anyone could see.

Ashyra Lee-Hall (8)
High View Primary School, Wallington

My Giant, Ferocious Monster

Under my bed,
I found a furry, ferocious monster!
It only had a head.
And it had arms,
Joined to its neck.
It was starting to greedily peck,
At my soft, large bed.

The very next morning,
It jumped into my bag quickly without a single warning!
It started to cause trouble,
And it was really starting to look horrible
My teacher loudly beckoned
'What's all the trouble?'
I told her what had happened,
Just before I awakened,
And realised it was all a dream.
Or was it?

Thive Thevapalan (8)
High View Primary School, Wallington

Guess What Was Under My Bed?

No wonder I heard snoring in the night,
That was as loud as a frightening lion.
I looked under my bed and was shocked at the sight,
And he told me his name was Ryan.

Who? A miniature, adorable monster,
Sucking his thumb, so sweet!
Suddenly he called me bonkers,
And then jumped out by my feet.

Soon after that, we became best friends,
And we went for a midnight walk.
We went to the park, that's not where it ends . . .
Without warning another one popped out,
It was his mum (Leigh!) (No doubt.)

They both screamed and burst into tears,
'I'm so glad to see you again!'
We had a celebration so we said, 'Cheers!'
But then they left, and had to go home, (that was small as a den!)

Every week they came to visit me,
But I will never forget Ryan and Leigh!

Jessica Heyne (9)
High View Primary School, Wallington

The Greedy Plump Monster

The monster came hastening in,
His face as chubby as thick snow,
He stomped into my infinitesimal room,
And shouted as loud as possible,
'I'm hungry and I want you!'
His face was sweaty and he was dribbling like mad,
But the one thing that scared me,
Were his humongous, sharp teeth

He was as hirsute as a furry pet,
But he was as angry as a lion!
The first thing I wanted to do,
Was to scream and shout for help!
This was an overweight greedy monster,
Who was hungry and wanted some food,
And what he was hoping for the most,
Was me,
For his dinner!

How could he be so offensive?
So slimy and sloppy too!
But one thing I couldn't forget,
Was to shout for help and jump!
So that was exactly what I did,
And my mum came running in,
Bashing the monster with her pan,
And that was when we found him on the floor,
Lying as still as someone dead,
So that was when we celebrated,
The death of the Greedy Plump Monster!

Israa Gulzar (9)
High View Primary School, Wallington

The Hole

It was a normal day,
On Wesley Street,
I was strolling down the road,
Listening to a beat.

Then I saw a thing
Coming from a hole,
A long slimy line,
As black as coal.

I went to investigate,
The strange sighting,
I gazed in amazement,
Looking down at the thing.

My eyes as big as dishes,
I couldn't believe what I'd seen,
It had gleaming blue eyes,
And its skin was light green.

It came to grab me,
By the hand,
And I screamed so much,
I was as loud as a marching band.

I wriggled and waggled,
My way out of the thing,
So I would stop all,
Screaming and shouting.

I ran back home,
As fast as a car,
My legs were worn out,
Because I'd ran so far.

I leapt into the kitchen,
I told my mum,
But all she said was,
'Don't be silly son.'

William Savill (1)
High View Primary School, Wallington

The Attic Loving Bill

I looked under my uninteresting bed,
Hurt my head,
And said to myself, there's nothing there.
So I looked in the bath
And I cried with a laugh
For what I had seen could not be real
As it looked like a orange peel
But of course it was a monster!

He cried, 'I'm Bill,
Can we go to the attic?'
I was puzzled at why he would want to go there,
But I didn't care,
So we did.

We played hide-and-seek,
Luckily he wouldn't peek,
And then I couldn't find him,
I looked everywhere but brilliant Bill was gone.
The next morning I looked in the bath,
I could see a strange orange mark,
Was it him?

Elizabeth Grinham (8)
High View Primary School, Wallington

The Monster In The Closet

When I went to rest my head,
Upon my soft and silky bed,
'What's that noise?' I suddenly said.
Then I checked,
Nothing under my bed.
I checked my pencil case,
But there was only lead.
I checked my closet and there was he,
A huge gigantic monster with tea!

Then he gently said to me, 'Would you like to have tea with the Queen?'
So I said yes and off we went,

The Queen was nice and let us in,
We went inside and drank some tea,
We ate cake, which surprised me,
After a while, we had to flee
So off we went my monster and me
We flew through the sky and landed safely.

Poppy (9)
High View Primary School, Wallington

My Pet Monster

Once there was a monster,
His fur was as white as snow,
He used to laugh and be joyful,
But that was a very long time ago.

Now he roams around the village,
With his furry head hung low,
Then one day he looked right down,
And saw a little boy below,

The boy brought him to his house one day,
They had a lot of fun,
They played on the swing and they played on the slide,
They even had a race, but of course the monster won!

When the day was nearly over,
A thunderstorm came along,
But the monster wouldn't come inside,
Something was going to go wrong.

The boy ran towards the monster,
He brought him some water inside a cup,
The boy got worried in case he was hurt,
After some twists and turns the monster got up . . .

'I've learnt my lesson!' the monster exclaimed,
'Always do as you're told.'
The boy and the monster went back inside,
They went outside day after day but always remembered to come inside
When it got cold!

Minhal Rafiq (11)
High View Primary School, Wallington

Cute But Evil

Red and fuzzy that is what it looked like,
Sapphire blue eyes sparkling in the sun,
Riding a bike,
Looks awfully like my son,
it called me Papa,
I called it Hopa.

A pedestrian strolled by,
Hopa ate him whole,
Like an evil mastermind,
He knew he must get all the world's souls,

He approached me with an evil look in his eyes,
I made a quick remark,
It went like 'Bye bye'
Hopa followed me through the park,
He even slammed through solid bark,
And I knew that this was the end.

I ran into the open to meet my destiny,
But instead of being dead,
I was in for something even more that I dread . . .

Gerald Ako-Otchere (11)
High View Primary School, Wallington

The Friendly Monster

One day I opened my window and saw a merry monster there,
He was trying to look good so he was brushing his hair,
When he saw me he started to blush,
And because he was frightened he dropped his brush!

I whispered 'Hello,' and he told me back,
'Hello, my name is Jack.'
'I am Alice,' I said with a smile
'Nice to meet you,' he said after a while.

We went out for the day and had a lovely time,
We had ice cream and mine was flavoured lime
When he said he had to go I wanted to cry,
But instead I said, 'Come another time'
He said he would and we are best friends now,
But then he disappeared with a bow.

Alice Johnson (9)
High View Primary School, Wallington

The Unexpected

It was a gloomy day,
I was at my grandma's for a stay,
There was a petrifying sound!
I thought it was underground,
Do you know what it is?
I decided to go down.

It looked like someone was moving,
I thought it was my mum and went straight in,
I saw a gigantic blue hairy monster,
I screeched with fright,
The monster screeched back,
He put his finger on his lips and hid,

Days kept going like this and I decided it was too much,
So I followed the monster and said 'Hello,'
That started an amazingly long conversation,
After that we got along well,
I found out I was friends with a big scary and hairy friend!

Adil Walji (10)
High View Primary School, Wallington

Making Monsters

Based On 'Making Monsters' By Gavin Stewart

Riogla the monster
I made up last week
A monster so scary
I'm now losing sleep!

My monster has . . .
A body like a rhino
Eyes as dark as night
He has skin as scaly as a snake
And he has feet as furry as a lion

My monster is . . .
As scary as a dragon
As loud as fireworks
As clever as Einstein
As smelly as a bin
As frightening as lightning

Riogla the monster
I made up last week
A monster so scary
I'm now losing sleep!

Isabella Woolcott (8)
St Cuthbert Mayne Catholic Junior School, Hemel Hempstead

Making Monsters

Based On 'Making Monsters' By Gavin Stewart

Gruff, the monster
I made up last week,
A monster so scary
I'm now losing sleep!

Evelyn Tess
Kempson xxx

My monster has . . .
He has nails like swords!
And horns like a pin,
He has feet like a penguin,
A belly that looks like a balloon,
And his face is white as snow.

My monster is . . .
He is as spooky as a witch,
And as smelly as a pair of socks.
He is as naughty as a naughty teacher,
But he is my golden treasure.

Evelyn Kempson (7)
St Cuthbert Mayne Catholic Junior School, Hemel Hempstead

The Undertaker Day

Based On 'Making Monsters' By Gavin Stewart

I wake up in California
I hear a knock on the door
I open it
It's this 9ft 2 muscular beast,
I go downstairs for breakfast.

We go out to do bungee jumping,
Then we try out driving sports cars
Then we have a BBQ for lunch
We go to the rock climbing centre
And we play football
Then we go on the Xbox 360
We have McDonald's for dinner
Then he wants to take over the world!

Tadiwa Musuka (10)
St Cuthbert Mayne Catholic Junior School, Hemel Hempstead

Making Monsters

Based On 'Making Monsters' By Gavin Stewart

Oshbosh the monster
I made up last week
A monster so scary
I'm now losing sleep.

My monster has
A body like a balloon
Eyes as big as a bowling ball
He has skin as scaly as a snake
Feet like claws of a cheetah
A tail like an arrow.

My monster is
As scary as a dragon
As loud as a trumpet
As clever as a scientist
As smelly as a skunk.

Oshbosh the monster
I made up last week
A monster so scary
I'm now losing sleep.

Stephen McDonnell (7)
St Cuthbert Mayne Catholic Junior School, Hemel Hempstead

Me And Dynamite

Based On 'Making Monsters' By Gavin Stewart

One day I met a black gooey monster with dynamite in his stomach.
He said, 'Dynamite is my name,' in a deep voice.
'I might look evil, but I'm kind,' in a sarcastic way.
'Although you might look evil, you are nice.
Do you want to go to the park?'
He said, 'Yes.'
So we played on the swings, joyfully.
Then I asked Dynamite a question, 'Do you want to take over the world?'
He said 'Yes,' in a shouty way.
And they took over the world . . .

Jack Sullivan (9)
St Cuthbert Mayne Catholic Junior School, Hemel Hempstead

Making Monsters

Based On 'Making Monsters' By Gavin Stewart

Zop the monster
I made up last week.
A monster so scary
I'm now losing sleep . . .

My monster has . . .
A body like a hard solid rock
Eyes as scary as a skeleton
He has skin like a snake
Feet like a giant dinosaur.

My monster is . . .
As scary as a vampire
As loud as a lion
As clever as an eagle
As smelly like a smelly toilet.

Jacob McDaid-Topping (8)
St Cuthbert Mayne Catholic Junior School, Hemel Hempstead

Making Monsters

Based On 'Making Monsters' By Gavin Stewart

Shracolob the monster
I made up last week
A monster so scary
I'm now losing sleep.

My monster has . . .
A body like shaggy fur from a lion's mane.
He's as dark as night.
Skin as bumpy as a snake under his fur.
Feet like dragon's claws.
A tail like a shaggy brick.

My monster is . . .
As scary as a dragon
As loud as a tiger's roar
As clever as a scientist
As smelly as a sock.

Tilly Morrissey (7)
St Cuthbert Mayne Catholic Junior School, Hemel Hempstead

Making Monsters

Based On 'Making Monsters' By Gavin Stewart

Ering the monster
I made up last week.
A monster so scary
I'm now losing sleep
My monster has a body
Round as a football
Face like an eagle
Feet like vampire feet
My monster is like a dragon
As loud as a dinosaur
As clever as a scientist
As smelly as an old sock.

James Doherty (7)
St Cuthbert Mayne Catholic Junior School, Hemel Hempstead

Making Monsters

Based On 'Making Monsters' By Gavin Stewart

The One Eyed monster
I made up last week
A monster so scary
I'm now losing sleep . . . !

My monster has . . .
A body like a hairy lion
eyes as big as a bowling ball
He has skin as prickly as holly
Feet like nails.

Monster is . . .
As scary as thunder
As loud as a tiger
As clever as a cheetah
As smelly as a bin
As frightening as a scorpion.

Mia Edwards (7)
St Cuthbert Mayne Catholic Junior School, Hemel Hempstead

Making Monsters

Based On 'Making Monsters' By Gavin Stewart

Sharaling the monster
I made up last week
A monster so scary
I'm losing my sleep . . . !

My monster has
A body like a rectangle
Eyes like an eagle
Sharp as diamonds.

My monster is
As scary as a lion
As smelly like a bin
As loud an an elephant.

Sharaling the monster
I made up last week
A monster so scary
I'm losing my sleep.

Nigel Vincent (8)
St Cuthbert Mayne Catholic Junior School, Hemel Hempstead

The Furbie

Based On 'Making Monsters' By Gavin Stewart

There's a beast living far away,
And it lives in a cave,
You can steal its jewels if you dare,
But you might get burned by its fiery hair,
It's even bigger than a bear,
It will probably poison you with snake venom,
It may look cute, but it's a real beast,
Can you guess her name?
That's right it's Furbie!

Katie Mackay-Grant (9)
St Cuthbert Mayne Catholic Junior School, Hemel Hempstead

My Little Nigel-Fred

Based On 'Making Monsters' By Gavin Stewart

I met him in the playground, he's fluffy, fun and red.
And when I knelt down to greet him, he said, 'Hi I'm Nigel-Fred!'
I took him for an ice cream and pushed him on the swing,
We went on the zip line when I felt i had a wing.

We skipped home together, happily hand in hand,
We stopped at the sweet shop, we were the jolliest in the land.
I snuck him through the back door, we crept up the stairs,
We were as quiet as mice, then I flumped in my chair.
I made him a little pillow, he slept in a cardboard box
We had a midnight feast, we were as sly as a fox
He always sleeps under my cosy bed
I still have him now my little Nigel-Fred.

Lara Baxendale (9)
St Cuthbert Mayne Catholic Junior School, Hemel Hempstead

Making Monsters

Based On 'Making Monsters' By Gavin Stewart

Manky the monster
I made up last week
A monster so scary
I'm now losing sleep . . . !

My monster has . . .
A body like a fat football
Eyes as big as the sun
Skin as green as slime.

My monster is . . .
As scary as a lion
As loud as a trumpet
As clever as a scientist
As smelly as a stinky sock.

Manky the monster
I made up last week
A monster so scary
I'm now losing sleep . . . !

Molly Sears (7)
St Cuthbert Mayne Catholic Junior School, Hemel Hempstead

Aston The Monster

Based On 'Making Monsters' By Gavin Stewart

Aston the monster
I made up last week
A monster so scary
I'm now losing sleep!

My monster has a body
Like a plate of mushy peas
He has skin as hairy as a gorilla

My monster is
As scary as a ghost
As loud as plate getting hammered
As brainy as a scientist
As smelly like an old sock.

Aston the monster
I made up last week
A monster so scary
I'm now losing sleep!

Max Dolt (-3)
St Cuthbert Mayne Catholic Junior School, Hemel Hempstead

Hell Hound

Based On 'Making Monsters' By Gavin Stewart

There once was a hound
Called a Hell Hound
Which was born in a fire.
Its skin was black
Its eyes were as blue as the sky,
Yet still as red on fire,
His teeth were as sharp as a blade from a knife,
With blood on them,
The hound infects everything it touches.
When a man came along, the hound attacked him
Then someone's car overheated and the noise scared the hound
Never to be seen again.

Luis Beattie (10)
St Cuthbert Mayne Catholic Junior School, Hemel Hempstead

Making Monsters

Based On 'Making Monsters' By Gavin Stewart

Zoockroo
I made up last week
A monster so scary
I'm now losing sleep . . . !

My monster has . . .
A body kick as scary as can be
Eyes as hot as lava
He has skin as furry as can be
Feet like a sharp dagger.

My monster is . . .
As scary as a massive bear
As loud as a roar
As clever as a scientist
As smelly like a dustbin.

Annabelle Hexter (7)
St Cuthbert Mayne Catholic Junior School, Hemel Hempstead

Sneaky And Me

Based On 'Making Monsters' By Gavin Stewart

One day I met a monster
He was little, indestructible and dark blue,
He came from a prison,
He had no friends,
Except for me
We went to London
Late at night,
We went to steal the precious crown jewels
Which were as sparkly as diamonds.
Secret security saw us but Sneaky scared them away
We managed to grab the jewels and we sprinted away.

Conor East (10)
St Cuthbert Mayne Catholic Junior School, Hemel Hempstead

Making Monsters

Based On 'Making Monsters' By Gavin Stewart

Spicey
I made up last week
A monster so scary
I'm now losing sleep . . . !

My monster has . . .
A body like a creepy crawler
Eyes as prickly as a wolf's
He has skin as a snake's
Feet like a wolf.

My monster is . . .
As scary as a lion
As loud as an elephant
As clever as a dog
As smelly like a bin.

Spicey
I made up last week
A monster so scary
I'm now losing sleep . . . !

Maddison (7)
St Cuthbert Mayne Catholic Junior School, Hemel Hempstead

The Big Fluffy And Hairy Monster

Based On 'Making Monsters' By Gavin Stewart

Ross the monster
Stamps in the jungle
Fluffy and hairy,
Huge and cute.
Don't be scared, I am a friendly monster.
They invited him for tea
He had a big chocolate cake for tea.

Emily Nekouzad (11)
St Cuthbert Mayne Catholic Junior School, Hemel Hempstead

Making Monsters

Based On 'Making Monsters' By Gavin Stewart

I made up last week
A monster so scary
I'm now losing sleep . . . !

My monster has . . .
A body like a balloon
Eyes as sharp as an eagle
He has skin as scaly as a dinosaur
Feet like penguins

My monster is
As scary as a poisonous snake
As loud as a lion
As clever as Mrs Young
As smelly like an old shoe.

Jazmyne Leach (8)
St Cuthbert Mayne Catholic Junior School, Hemel Hempstead

Making Monsters

Based On 'Making Monsters' By Gavin Stewart

Hutchitch the monster
I made up last week
A monster so scary
I'm now losing sleep . . . !

My monster
A body like a rugby ball
Eyes as big as a balloon
He has skin as scaly as a snake
Feet sharp like a platypus

My monster is . . .
As scary as a dinosaur
As loud as a lion
As clever as a wolf
As smelly as a sock
That hasn't been washed for five years.

Jermaine Allen (8)
St Cuthbert Mayne Catholic Junior School, Hemel Hempstead

The Day Of Panic

Based On 'Making Monsters' By Gavin Stewart

On my way home I opened my door,
I heard something move in the kitchen,
So I went outside to see what was happening,
I heard something in the tree, like it was rattling.

I saw a multicoloured monster
Or is it maybe just me?
It tried to chase me,
It made a sound like a bee.

I tried to run but it overtook me and pounced,
But it fell down and bounced.
It was a very scary monster that was dangerous and fast
Maybe it could watch me through present and past.

By now it had probably lifted to space,
But I had already called people to get on the case.
I also told them I needed a lot of shields,
So we could cover the Earth before it got peeled,
By now it was in space trying to ruin the Earth
But we had already put shields there.

It got so frustrated that it started dropping bombs,
But the bombs did nothing and just hit the floor like an anchor.
It blew him up, his friends were mad,
He had many friends, that were sad.

Kenechukwu (KK) Okereke (9)
St Cuthbert Mayne Catholic Junior School, Hemel Hempstead

Monster

Based On 'Making Monsters' By Gavin Stewart

As loud as a tiger
As creepy as a snake
Looking at his victim
His tasty victim
Munch!
And he was gone

Running around
Smashing, bashing,
Turning everything
Upside down.
The people shouted 'Stop!'
The monster sniffed, growled
And ate everyone in sight.

Weeks gone
Months gone
Until one day
He was gone.

Yippee, yippee!
Everyone shouted
But where did he go?
Where did he come from?
Nobody knows.

Oliver Saunders (11)
St Cuthbert Mayne Catholic Junior School, Hemel Hempstead

The Big Fight In The Dark!

Based On 'Making Monsters' By Gavin Stewart

There was a creeper called Skurch,
Who lived on a mountain called Burch,
He comes out at night,
To give people a fright,
Then retreats back to his cave with all his might.
Then one night I found a sword
In my cupboard and go and fight Skurch
Up on Burch.
Skurch is powerful and very clever
So it is going to be hard to pull his lever.
I fight and fight with all my might
But Skurch steals my sword and my kite.
I punch Skurch 15 times before he disappears
And my family have munch for lunch.

William Spencer (9)
St Cuthbert Mayne Catholic Junior School, Hemel Hempstead

The Goo Monsters

Based On 'Making Monsters' By Gavin Stewart

I was at my friend's house and I heard a big explosion.
Then there was loads of motion.
I saw a monster
It didn't look like a lobster.
It said to let me in.
I said no because you're a goo monster.
It slithered under the door,
And chased me to the top floor.
It found a toy,
It was a picture of a boy.
I gave it to him,
He didn't put it in the bin,
And we became friends.

Tao Heron (9)
St Cuthbert Mayne Catholic Junior School, Hemel Hempstead

Getting A Monster Dog

Based On 'Making Monsters' By Gavin Stewart

Today I am going to get a dog.
The small orange dog who lives in a log.

I'm a monster, I am, it's time to choose
That one, it's name is Foos with a yellow tum
I love it Mum
But the name is nasty
I'll call you Fizzy
My aunt is going to love you, her name is Cizzy

I love my dog,
I'll put him on my blog
We have a cat
We found her in a hat
But that's a whole different story.

Sarah Wilkins-Richardson (9)
St Cuthbert Mayne Catholic Junior School, Hemel Hempstead

My Monster Boomer

Based On 'Making Monsters' By Gavin Stewart

One day I came out of school,
When suddenly I heard a rustle in the bush.
Then it came out of the bush,
And I grabbed him.
I put him in my bag when no one was looking.
I went on the bus, my bag was shaking.
I finally got home, he flew out of my bag,
I saw him, he looked like a boomerang.
I asked him what his name was,
He said Boomer.
It was soon teatime,
I was taking some of my carrots under the table.
After a while, I went to bed,
Boomer now sleeps under the bunk bed.

Joseph Fairhurst (9)
St Cuthbert Mayne Catholic Junior School, Hemel Hempstead

The Ogerous Dynamite Story

Based On 'Making Monsters' By Gavin Stewart

He was born when the volcano erupted,
He is red and fiery hot.
He is sly and 9 foot 5.
Which makes him as tall as the Eiffel Tower.
Just within 5 seconds he could kill a person.
So one day he decided to rule Africa and Antarctica,
He got to Antarctica and nobody is there.
He freezes.
Half a month later, he unfreezes and then he went to Africa.
In Africa the plan doesn't work out so well.
Half an hour later, most people in Johannesburg were fighting him.
About 5 hours later the monster was so beaten down he was killed.
That was the end of Ogerous Dynamite!

Daniel Hosier (10)
St Cuthbert Mayne Catholic Junior School, Hemel Hempstead

The Lonely Monster

Based On 'Making Monsters' By Gavin Stewart

In a beautiful sunny day,
There was a lonely monster
Going on his way.
He was blue as the sky,
And red as the fire.
I felt sorry for the monster
Nobody wanted to play with him.
I showed up and asked to play
He was as happy as the sun.
We played all morning.
What happened he became my pet.

Kaze Sinzinkayo (6)
St Cuthbert Mayne Catholic Junior School, Hemel Hempstead

A Day Out With My Monster

Based On 'Making Monsters' By Gavin Stewart

There was once a monster called Fuzzle Bom
He was extremely cute, speedy and fuzzy
I was walking to Buckingham Palace and met him.

We started walking together
Hearing the birds chirp sweetly
And feeling the gloomy mist roll into my face gently.

We were seeing the tops of Buckingham Palace as we went
Then I got the taste of rain, as i dipped my tongue out.
I was getting nervous, teeth chattering as the snow started to fall.

We were there finally going through the doors of Buckingham Palace.
We went upstairs silently.
We were there saying hello to the Queen.
It felt amazing.

Finally and sadly the chat was over
We walked back home.

Lily Hanlon (9)
St Cuthbert Mayne Catholic Junior School, Hemel Hempstead

The Slimy, Ugly, Fussy Monster

Based On 'Making Monsters' By Gavin Stewart

The slimy, ugly, fussy monster got in a taxi
to go see the Queen.
He was going for lunch with her.
When he got out the taxi everyone ran away,
He tried to tell them he was nice.
But none of them listened.
When he got to the Queen's palace,
He told them he was having lunch with the Queen
But sadly they didn't believe him
So he started to walk away when the Queen let him in.

Katie Gallagher (10)
St Cuthbert Mayne Catholic Junior School, Hemel Hempstead

What Are You . . .

Based On 'Making Monsters' By Gavin Stewart

I wonder what you are?
Pink and blue.
As I walked through the torrential rain
As it dripped on the windowpane.
Its roar shattered my ear,
That's a fear.
He acted like Hulk and broke stuff.
Suddenly he disappeared.
I wish I could see him again.

This very day I met his brothers
It was much worse
Because I had to give back a purse.
But it was fun.

Jack (10)
St Cuthbert Mayne Catholic Junior School, Hemel Hempstead

Fridge Monster

Based On 'Making Monsters' By Gavin Stewart

Once upon a time
I woke up on a Saturday morning.
I went to get my breakfast
I opened the fridge door
And then I saw a monster . . .
Then jumped out
Trashed the house.
Smash!
Bang!
Crack!
12am I'm playing football
I don't know if he is coming back.
The next day I saw him in my bath.
I said, 'Let's go swimming.'

Daniel Power (10)
St Cuthbert Mayne Catholic Junior School, Hemel Hempstead

Monster Poem

Based On 'Making Monsters' By Gavin Stewart

One day, out of the corner of my eye
I saw a monster.
He was angry, hairy, chubby, ginormous and infectious.
He walked down the street,
To Buckingham Palace.
He met the Queen,
He tried to kill her,
But she was too good at martial arts,
But the monster ducked at the first kick the Queen took.
But she did her famous trick,
That she hasn't done in eternal life,
It worked,
And the monster died,
With shame,
And embarrassment.

Haydn Sears (10)
St Cuthbert Mayne Catholic Junior School, Hemel Hempstead

A Day In The Life Of Freak Face

Freak Face lives in the wood,
Freak Face is very, very good,
Freak Face goes for a walk,
Freak Face starts to talk.
'I am hungry,' he moans,
Until he bumps into the telephone.
He talks on and on and on,
Until the answerer is gone.

Freak Face lives in the wood,
Freak Face is very, very good,
Freak Face is scared of mice,
When he sees one, he eats rice.
He stays outside all day long,
And when night comes, he's all but gone.

Isabelle Haywood (9) & Bethany Nancarrow (10)
St. Mary's Junior School, Oxted

Silly Milly Monster

Silly Milly Monster went for a walk
Soon she gets tired and sits in a tree.

Silly Milly Monster likes to have a talk
Soon she gets bored, so she comes and finds me.

Silly Milly Monster tries to chew a fork
Soon she goes to Sainsbury's and buys a spring bean
And buys one, get one free.

So I took them home in a paper bag
And had a load of peas.

Olivia Andrews (9)
St. Mary's Junior School, Oxted

The Monster Of Fuzz!

Far, far away,
In the land of Guzz,
children snuggled in their beds,
Unaware of Fuzz.

He hides behind doors,
Under bridges and on moors,
He dines on bones and goo,
Do you eat that too?

His tongue shoots out,
Really, really fast,
Like the wind,
Going against a sailing mast.

So if you live in Guzz, hold onto your hair,
So if you live in Guzz, beware, beware, beware!

Sam Oxlade (9)
St. Mary's Junior School, Oxted

That's Me

I am tiny,
I am slimy,
I am frightening,
I am brightening,
I am dangerous,
I am horrendous,
These are all my family's names!
They also describe me, all my fine looks,
But everyone teases me, I always read books.
My body is tiny, my body is slimy,
My eyes can be frightening, my eyes can be brightening.
My claws are dangerous, my claws are horrendous,
And yes, my name is Tiny Monster!

Naomi Webb (10)
St. Mary's Junior School, Oxted

Fuzzy McMuzzy

Fuzzy McMuzzy is a busy buzzy monster,
He's always up to mischief when our backs are turned.
He eats pineapples which make him extra good,
He sometimes eats a bunch of grapes which also make him bad, extra bad.
And when I say bad, I mean really bad.
And when he eats pineapples and a bunch of grapes,
He gets brain freeze and goes to sleep for half an hour,
Snore, snore zzzz.
Fuzzy McMuzzy has just woken up.
All he can see is a big cop, in trouble with the law,
All he says is that you're a big bore.
This doesn't go down with the law,
He was sitting quiet,
He said, 'Shhhh and be quiet.'

Joe Davies (9)
St. Mary's Junior School, Oxted

Jobs, Friends And Lands Known By Bob

Bob has a job
Looking after baby blobs.

He flips them up,
He drops them down,
When he does he wears a big, soft gown.

He has a friend called Gob,
Who has the same old job,
Who lives in the land of Mob.

He has another friend called Fuzz,
Who lives in the land of Guzz,
And he goes *buzz, buzz, buzz.*

And last of all, Bob,
lives in the land of Glob!

Tom Davies (9)
St. Mary's Junior School, Oxted

Google The Magical Monster

If you tickle his tummy, he gets upset
He looks like a dinosaur
He acts like an apple core
He likes eating metal and copper and glass
He doesn't lie in bed, he sleeps in the grass.

Laurence Underwood (9)
St. Mary's Junior School, Oxted

Google The Magical Monster

If you tickle his tummy, he gets upset
He looks like a dinosaur
He acts like an apple core
he likes eating metal and copper and glass
He doesn't lie in bed, he sleeps in the grass.

Joe Baker (9)
St. Mary's Junior School, Oxted

The True Story Of Bruce Bogey

Bruce Bogey is my name
Bruce Bogey is my game
Bruce Bogey goes to dance
Bruce Bogey tries to prance
Bruce Bogey climbs a tree
Bruce Bogey can't find me
Bruce Bogey goes for a pee
Bruce Bogey that's me.

Isabel Fricker (9)
St. Mary's Junior School, Oxted

Roary Tangy-Fastic

Roary Tangy-Fastic
Is made of elastic
And wears Pampers
He also eats campers
And wins lots of hampers
He never sleeps
And likes to keep
Everything he gets
He has lots of pets
He likes to talk
And also stalks
Lots of people
Then he went to London
and got lost in the Dungeon
Forever and ever . . .

Ellie D'Alessandro (9), Tara (10) & Sarah (11)
St. Mary's Junior School, Oxted

What I Am

I am cuddly,
I live where it's puddly
I am sweet
But not neat
I am titch
And live in a ditch
I am daft
I hate having baths
I want some friends
With pet hens
I don't fit in
I'm like a bin
I love milkshakes
With some cakes
But most of all I like . . .
You.

Amber Crabtree-Cusick & Francesca Evans (10)
St. Mary's Junior School, Oxted

Razoo's Drink

My monster's name is Razoo
And lives up in our attic
He's not at all quiet
In fact he's pretty static!

The other day I saw him
Messing about by the kitchen table
I asked him what he's doing
He just carried on plugging in cables
He took all the food out the cupboards
Which really was a sight
Then this massive noise came on
Which gave me quite a fright.

Fruit went up the cupboard doors
And up and around the walls
Our kitchen's now mayhem
Fruit went through the halls.

Then Razoo let out a sign and said
'I think it's nearly done'
He gave it to me and said, 'Drink.'
This liquid weighed a ton.

I took a sip of this drink
It really was delicious
Then some funny things happened
Which made me quite suspicious.

I started to grow a tail
Some ears and some fur
I began to bark and roar
Then let out a purr
I turned into a monster
Then . . . Mum walked in!

Rose Wood (10)
St Mary Star Of The Sea Roman Catholic Primary School, St Leonards-On-Sea

Flossie

I went to the candyfloss stall.
She was waving at me,
With Her cloud-like body, her neon eyes.
She was different compared to others
She giggled softly,
My eyes grew wider,
'Mine!' I shouted.

I brought her back
She asked for sugar.
We were out of sugar.
'Edible glitter?'
She made a glitter ring
And pulled me inside.
Little did I know about
Our big adventure.

We land in a place called Candy Kingdom
With candy cane trees
And butterscotch lakes.
There were candy stalls at every corner.
Plain lands of hundreds and thousands.
Bang in the centre sat the Ice Cream Palace,
Where Flossie sat happily.

'Bye!'
Then Flossie faded.

Sinnead Singson (10)
St Mary Star Of The Sea Roman Catholic Primary School, St Leonards-On-Sea

The Blooming Flower

High up in the tallest tower,
There's a flower waiting to bloom.
Sitting beside it is,
A monster named Zoom,
He zooms around,
With his glasses so round,
he waits all day, he waits all night,
Until the flower starts to bloom!
It sparkles and shimmers, at night it glimmers,
And the monster starts to zoom.
All the way to Sugar Island.
Full of candy cane trees,
Oozing, melted chocolate rivers,
Strawberry snakes as they slither,
On the ground as they eat cherry bon-bon
We'll go to the candy store on Monday
Now it's time to go to the funfair
Fun day
In the middle there is a castle
Full of gummy bears and marshmallows.
But again Geek 'O' Zoom flies away
Neverland, Shopping Land and Food Land,
But from his adventures Geek 'O' Zoom
Always zoomed to his flower.
Who sparkles and shimmers.
All day and
All night, I'll never forget him.

Janel Manenclang (11)
St Mary Star Of The Sea Roman Catholic Primary School, St Leonards-On-Sea

Burning The Stars Away

I warned you once
But who would listen?
I am monster
I am different

I warned you twice
I begged and begged
But it didn't help
More and more
Day by day,
Going away.

My family died before my eyes
Every day one star would fade away.

The night turned darker than any nightmare
The days turned gloomy
And the people so moody.

But you kept on going
Killing, killing, killing us
There was millions of us but now sadly only one
And only one star that kept the light.

I couldn't fight
Any longer
I gave up
I surrendered
And then I realised
I was no monster.

One time in history I saw
People turning into monsters
And monsters turning into humans
With hearts as warm as fire.

Elizabeth Orden (10)
St Mary Star Of The Sea Roman Catholic Primary School, St Leonards-On-Sea

The Earth And Sky

When dawn is rising
Something happens, something surprising.
A little dragon rises from his bed,
A little blue horn,
And a body coated in red.
He jumps on the stars really high,
When he falls down he wails and cries.
One day he asked himself,
'If I were like rain,
That joins up the Earth and sky,
Could I join up two hearts?'
Curiously he went down to Earth,
Where he met a young boy.
He and the boy were best of friends,
But one day it came to an end,
A black car came speeding down,
The boy was in the middle of the road,
His face turned into a frown,
'Go run!'
Roared the little dragon.
Bang!
The little dragon was draped in blood.
His eyes were sealed, never to be revealed.
The stars mourned at this loss,
The dragon was their master, their boss.
The stars formed a shape of a dragon.
A blazing fire lifted from the dragon's heart and went up.
From above the boy heard a cry,
The dragon had done it,
He joined up two hearts, like the Earth and sky.

Alen Geevarghese (11)
St Mary Star Of The Sea Roman Catholic Primary School, St Leonards-On-Sea

Sticky Things

He is such a sticky thing
I see him when I sleep
He is partly a ghost
And he is always funny
He eats candy all day
And has vegetables for a treat
He goes around town at night stealing candy
Yum, yum, yummy, yum
He runs around for fun
With candyfloss in his hand
He has bits stuck in his fur
He is called Candyfloss.

Bailey Vice (11)
St Mary Star Of The Sea Roman Catholic Primary School, St Leonards-On-Sea

Bob

When I went to the London Dungeons,
Something very peculiar happened.
I met a monster named Bob,
How he got there I don't know,
But he was a friend, not a foe.
I took him to the park,
And he ate all the ice cream
The expenses made me scream
He scared all the children off the swings,
He couldn't find another friend,
But it was not the end.
He taught me how to make a spaceship,
And together we flew to Mars.
But then he told me he had to go
I was feeling very low,
But Bob came up with an idea,
At first I had great fear.
Now I'm living on Mars,
With my best friend Bob,
Eating corn on the cob.

Erika Body (9)
St Mary Star Of The Sea Roman Catholic Primary School, St Leonards-On-Sea

My Friend Mr Mastasio

There was a monster called Mastasio,
He comes from planet Zugaruba,
But Zugar for short,
He's very nice and likes to laugh,
But in some sort of snort,
And every night at five past twilight,
He sneaks inside my room.
And protects me from my nightmare,
About sudden death or doom!

Esmé Comer (9)
St Mary Star Of The Sea Roman Catholic Primary School, St Leonards-On-Sea

The Monster Wins The Race

There once was a monster
And nobody knew his name
But he got told to do the race
Just the same.

And on that night
He thought
About losing
And if he lost
Nobody would like him.

He lost all
The trials
And got scared
By his rivals
And . . .
The day of the race
Begun
And do you know what he did?

He won!

Daniel Hampton (9)
St Mary Star Of The Sea Roman Catholic Primary School, St Leonards-On-Sea

My Monster

Me and my monster,
The perfect pair
We stick together
Like glue
Me and her.

She is there when my eyes close
And when they open.
But nobody knows she's there
She is just our little secret.

She curls under my bed at night,
And plays in the woods in the day.
Oh how I love my monster
Me and her.

My monster was scared
She was lonely
But now I have her
And I don't ever want to let her go.

One day my monster will leave,
She won't play with me anymore.
I don't want those days to come
I want her to be my monster,
Now and forever more.

Lillie Rigby-Faux (10)
St Mary Star Of The Sea Roman Catholic Primary School, St Leonards-On-Sea

Burping Bert

My mum turns out the lights,
Then it's just me and the haunting night,
I count to ten and I hear a . . .
Burp,
Followed by a nasty slurp,
My heart is pounding,
My head is racing,
I sweat from head to toe,
'Boo!'
Out popped burping Bert with a purple body,
And brown spots all over (which really is dirt)
With terrible teeth and google eyes,
It gave me an awful surprise,
Burp!
He took me to the land where bedtime monsters roam,
Where trees were made of candyfloss,
And they sold ice cream on every corner,
Hills and hills with orange spots,
And trees with purple dots,
Bert and I played all day long,
And we became the best of friends.
Now every night when my mum turns out the light,
I count to ten and I hear a burp
Followed by a nasty slurp,
But this time I am not
frightened
Burp!

Kiera Davey (10)
St Mary Star Of The Sea Roman Catholic Primary School, St Leonards-On-Sea

A Monster Diary

A boy from planet Earth,
There I sat on his turf,
I flew up to his window,
He went on his pillow.
While I tapped on is window,
He was brave,
He got up to get a pill argh!
I went through the panes,
That was a pain.
Because his dad ran upstairs with a pitchfork.

Aneirin Goodman (10)
St Mary Star Of The Sea Roman Catholic Primary School, St Leonards-On-Sea

Bubbles

Bubbles went to the moon,
He said he would be back soon.
But now it is a mystery
As he is unfortunately history.
Now fuzzy, bouncy Bubbles stays upon the nasty, rock moon
Hoping for a night where all his dreams come true.
Bubbles smelled some cheese that lay upon a tree.
When Bubbles got some cheese, he ate it up.
Please I would like to see Bubbles again
As he is a very nice friend.

Hannah Andrews (8)
St Meryl School, Watford

Fish Cat That Was On The Beach

One day when I was walking on the beach
I saw the strangest monster
Ears like a squirrel
A pigeon like beak
Eats eels and fish
It's name was Fish Cat
She had a scary tail
And the scales shone on her neck.
We swam to the cave underwater
We ate fish fingers
We drank salty seawater
Fish Cat liked to eat
Fish Cat liked to swim
Fish Cat swam away that day
Was it all a dream?

Evie Bunker (9)
St Meryl School, Watford

A Day With The Pirate

Cloudy went to see the pirate ship,
He sat down on the white mat
And he ate a cake.
At last the pirate ship opened,
But suddenly the pirate ship sailed to the Queen!
There was beans and cream with strawberries.
Also cherries, jelly and ice cream.
Cloudy ate everything in a flash.

Paris Rice (8)
St Meryl School, Watford

Smelly Breath

He comes from an underwater house
His only friend is his squeaky pet mouse
I met him first in the boxing ring
Where his talent earns him money ch . . . ching!
But he boxes in a very odd way
He puts up his fists and starts to sway
He opens his mouth, and out comes his breath
And to his opponent this means death!
He took me for lunch with his boxing winnings
A Toby Carvery with all the trimmings
But Smelly Breath wanted even more cash
So back to the boxing ring we had to dash
The million pounds he wanted to claim
And I knew he'd put the other guy to shame
But just when I saw him receive first prize
The dream ended and I opened my eyes!

Malachi Kavanagh (8)
St Meryl School, Watford

Keven

Walking to school on the street
A monster I met, he was tall and he was hairy,
I thought he was a bit scary.
Did he want to eat me?
No he liked me.
He went to the park to have fun.
We smelled the grass
And we ate food.
Keven the monster got in a mood.

Natalie Fakhr (8)
St Meryl School, Watford

Ewwey Monster

One day I met the scissor hand beast in the park
And made friends with the hairy thing
Also we played games in the park
And then we went for hot, tasty food and a cold drink.
After we played more games.
in the afternoon we played volleyball on the beach.
Then it was a all a trick and killed.

Harry Edwards (8)
St Meryl School, Watford

A Day With The Queen

Fireball came from the top of the cliff
He had a wobbly antenna and orange fur.
I met him on his way to the Queen
And he was very keen.
So he went to the Queen.
And they had some kiwi.
Then Fireball went home.
The Queen wishes he could visit again.

Nedim Pasic (8)
St Meryl School, Watford

The Cuddly Monster

Cuddly sat on the blue mat and smelt his purple hat.
Cuddly sat on the wall and fell off them all!
He was the boss and cross.
He went on this adventure to make everyone smile.

Jack Mantrippe (8)
St Meryl School, Watford

Ugly The Monster

I met him in a cafe one day,
It was fun, we ate and ate.
We were still hungry.
We fancied fish.
There was no fish in stock,
So we went for a swim.
We soon found a young salmon,
Off we swam after the salmon.
Sitting at the table and in my tum.
Goody goody to the movies,
Popcorn and sweets and all sorts of treats.
Goodbye Ugly, I hope we meet again
Thanks for the things we did,
Goodnight, I'm going to bed.

Grace Bunker (9)
St Meryl School, Watford

Snee's Great Adventure In England

What was it? Nobody knows,
Where had it come from? Nobody goes,
I saw him when I was crossing the road,
Swish, swish, his tail flowed,
I brought him to school to scare my teacher,
But little did I know, in literacy, he had a special feature,
I brought him home to scare my sister,
But his claws gave her a blister,
When he left to where he himself lived (his home),
His tail still looked like it needed a comb!

Charlotte Vernon (8)
St Meryl School, Watford

Fire Horns Saves The World

I was on my way to play football,
My friends asked if they could play,
So we set off on our way there,
We saw a monster all cheery,
So we asked him if he wanted to play,
He said yes,
And at the end of the match
He said he was on a mission.

Hammaad Khan (9)
St Meryl School, Watford

Ugly Man

I met this monster on a ship.
He tried to skip.
He was born to take over the world.
He twirled.

He is from the planet Bamzuki
He had a pen called Suki
He has slime
He is a crime.

He could smell the fire from his shoes
He could hear the cows moos
He could feel the soft fluffy clouds
He could hear the circus clowns

He fails to take over both Earth and Bamzuki.

Alex Szalanski (8)
St Meryl School, Watford

Silly Billy

In a land unknown, there was a boy called Silly Billy
He was as red as chilli
Then one day there was a shout, 'Help! Help!'
There were people yelping.
The volcano is going to erupt
Then Silly Billy accidentally erupted his planet
And a piece fell off and landed in a swimming pool.
All the water landed on the volcano,
Suddenly it stopped erupting.

Neal Storhaug (9)
St Meryl School, Watford

Jemmy Jelly's Visit

On the way to school I met a monster
Who was an orange fool.
He wore a red bow tie.
For lunch he ate a pie.
My friend Kelly helped Jemmy Jelly fly a kite
But instead he had a bite!
'I will come back,' Jemmy Jelly said,
And flew away as fast as a lightning bolt,
He was gone.
'Will he come back?' I wondered and I walked home!

Daniel Hatcher (8)
St Meryl School, Watford

Zaple Who Came To Tea

Zaple came to see the strange looking me.
When he saw me he said, 'I want to eat!'
So when I went to the kitchen I fried some lovely chicken.
But when he smelt it, he said, 'Yuck, I don't want this!'
'Then go! Go away! Never come again,
Otherwise I will eat you up, because you're not my friend!'
So he never came back to his friend . . .

Shaan Nayee (8)
St Meryl School, Watford

Zapper Who Almost Took Over

I met Zapper at school
He tried to eat me, that was just wrong
Then I almost got shocked, naughty.
He lived in wires and he's Chinese,
He had horns like shark's teeth,
He wanted to take over the universe.
He was evil, also Zapper was ten foot!
Electric he was.
I decided to go with him.
He zapped people, we could smell burning people.
Plus he had spikes like teeth.
Red like fire, felt shocked.
Touch electric tasting Chinese saw dead people
I gasp, then we fought.
I won!

Harvey Wilkinson (9)
St Meryl School, Watford

Zap Zap The First Saved The World

Zap Zap The First heard there was an evil monster with hair that curled.
So Zap Zap decided to save the world,
I saw him at my open window,
He was made of playdough,
Also very very fast,
I think he came from the past.

Sophie Wilkes (9)
St Meryl School, Watford

The Monster Who Went To The Zoo

I'm scary hairy monster and I'm going to the zoo,
Do you like animals?
Yes I do
Zebras and monkeys one, two, three.
I love animals can't you see?
At the zoo I was walking my beagle and then down swooped
A great bald eagle.
As I walked into the dirty shop, it was so smelly, I had to hop.
As I eat my mouldy food, I saw someone in a grumpy mood.
When we took a trip on the Safari jeep,
We saw a cheetah do a big leap!
I was driving on my way home,
My monster said 'Phew' with a groan.

Bella Della-Savina (8)
St Meryl School, Watford

Me And My Monster Day Out

Me and my monster - fuzzy, furry and friendly as kind as can be.
He has no harm, he once helped a dog get to its barn.
Once me and my monster went out for tea,
And he was as well behaved as me!
He won the Nobel Prize, he must have - he never lies.
So that's why you can ask him for tea!
Then it's night,
I switched off the light,
And he turned back into my teddy bear.
And that was my monster day out.

Christian (7)
St Meryl School, Watford

A Day Out With My Monster

My monster came out of planet Fuzz for a day,
His best friend Crazy Fuzz also came to play,
We went on a train to London, where people did stare,
My monster smelt of strawberries, it must have been a scare.
His fur was as soft as pillows, as he got off the train,
We were going for a picnic, our hamper made it plain,
We sat on the gorgeous green grass, my monster and I,
Then we ate warm cheese pizzas, and looked up at the bright, blue sky.
Then my monster said, 'Now I have to zoom,'
I said, 'OK, but please come back soon.'

Lucia Della-Savina (10)
St Meryl School, Watford

A Day Out With Crazy Fuzz

My monster came out of planet Fuzz for the day,
Her best friend Fuzzball also came out to play,
We went on the train to Brighton Station,
Where the beach was ready for the whole nation,
It was a bright sunny day,
Where the sun came out, well it may!
We saw a space on the soft sand,
Where we saw a little rubber band,
We decided to walk to the sea,
My fuzzy monster and me.

Skye Narroway (9)
St Meryl School, Watford

Cutey!

I was walking home one day,
It was the 5th of May,
I saw this monster
Who looked like a funstar.

This monster looked as good as a hamster,
But the star sign is sporting Cancer,
She said her name was Cutey
And she's such a beauty.

This funny, fuzzy monster is so cute,
She is like a silver flute,
Cutey is so sociable,
And so negotiable.

Cutey is a little likeable monster,
She is caring, careful and kind.

Andrea Hutchison (9)
St Meryl School, Watford

A Day Out With Honey

I was walking along the street one day,
When a pink thing caught my eyes.
It was fluffy, fuzzy, furry and fun, just like a roller coaster
High in the sky!
I asked it what it was doing here, and it said to me,
'My name is Honey and I am a monster from the planet of Cuteness,
Don't you see?'
We walked along the street until we reached the park,
Then we stayed there until it got dark.
All of a sudden she said to me, 'I'm sorry but I have to leave,'
Then she gave me a great big smile, and waved bye bye into the sky!

Georgia Brass (10)
St Meryl School, Watford

Super Scary Monsters

Scary Eye Monster went on a craft,
When he went up the raft,
He giggled and laughed louder and louder,
He did this plan all by himself.
Also he went to the main controls with his crew,
And he set off the ship and went 'Woo hoo!'
The frightening, ferocious, freaky monster went and started the ship,
Captured the planets with his eye in a ball
He reached up high and tall
To get something from the fridge
As he was doing it to the last planet
There was a huge bang
It was a reflector shield
It hit the globe and went right in the field.
That was the end of the plans for Scary Eye Monster.

Brandon Kavanagh (9)
St Meryl School, Watford

A Reason To Be Scared

My monster is from planet Slick Slim
Which tops all the others

My monster is a dangerous, deadly Dracula
Which is the scariest ever.

My monster, the most disruptive, destroying,
Deadly, dangerous monster.

My monster will slick slim slim his way
Around the world.

When he is on his planet,
He hears the aeroplane zooming past.

Max Keegan (9)
St Meryl School, Watford

Devil Gigantosaurus Adventure

There lived a monster called Devil Gigantosaurus
He was half Devil and half Gigantosaurus.
He went to Zenus in his car
And while he was driving, he wanted to buy some chocolate bars.
When he landed, he landed from the sky,
At first everybody thought that it was a pie.
After that he walked around and met a dinosaur.
Then he saw a vicious moor.
Then he saw his family that he never knew,
And almost screamed and then he went 'Phew!'
After that he went back to the monster star,
And on the way he stopped at the bar.

Ethan Rice (9)
St Meryl School, Watford

Untitled

My robotic monster is the best
My monster is hairier than a chest
My monster is always strong
My monster is always powerful
My monster is scary and strong
My monster will never get scared
My monster friend is sociable but not negotiable
I know I'm a monster but I'm a hero
My monster will save the world.

Ari Khatri (9)
St Meryl School, Watford

Fizz Fluff Saves The Day

When I was walking to school,
Something cute and cuddly
Fell right in front of me,
Fizz Fluff was her name,
'Help me,' she said,
'Save my planet,
And my friend Rabbit.'

'Yes!' And we shot,
High into the sky,
Past cuddly clouds and shining stars.

We landed on Monster World,
The lasers were like rockets,
It was a disaster,
Fizz Fluff transferred her power into me,
We shot fizz lightning bolts and the aliens faded.

Natalie Parsons (9)
St Meryl School, Watford

Cutey

Once I found a monster
His name was Cutey Pie
He was very hairy and very fat
He lived in a tyre
His eyes were as shiny as wire
He went to school with me
How we were full of glee
What a feeling I had when he had to leave.

Skarlett-Eve Pope (8)
St Meryl School, Watford

Young Writers Information

We hope you have enjoyed reading this book and that you will continue to in the coming years.

If you're a young writer who enjoys reading and creative writing, or the parent of an enthusiastic poet or story writer, do visit our website www.youngwriters.co.uk. Here you will find free competitions, workshops and games, as well as recommended reads, a poetry glossary and our blog.

If you would like to order further copies of this book, or any of our other titles, then please give us a call or visit **www.youngwriters.co.uk.**

Young Writers
Remus House
Coltsfoot Drive
Peterborough
PE2 9BF
(01733) 890066 / 898110
info@youngwriters.co.uk